2013 ICD-10-CM and ICD-10-PCS Workbook

Mary Jo Bowie
MS, BS, AAS, RHIA, RHIT

Gail I. Smith
MA, RHIA, CCS-P

CENGAGE
Learning

**2013 ICD-10-CM and
ICD-10-PCS Workbook**
Mary Jo Bowie and Gail I. Smith

VP, GM, Skills & Product Planning:
Dawn Gerrain

Product Director: Stephen Helba

Product Team Manager: Rhonda Dearborn

Senior Director, Development: Marah
Bellegarde

Product Development Manager: Juliet Steiner

Content Developer: Lauren Whalen

Product Assistant: Courtney Cozzy

Executive Brand Manager: Wendy Mapstone

Senior Market Development Manager:
Nancy Bradshaw

Senior Production Director: Wendy Troeger

Production Manager: Andrew Crouth

Art and Cover Direction, Production
Management, and Composition:
PreMediaGlobal

Media Developer: William Overocker

Cover Image: © Norph/shutterstock

For product information and technology assistance, contact us at
Cengage Learning Customer & Sales Support, 1-800-354-9706.
For permission to use material from this text or product,
submit all requests online at **www.cengage.com/permissions.**
Further permissions questions can be e-mailed to
permissionrequest@cengage.com.

Library of Congress Control Number: 2013937079

ISBN-13: 978-1-133-60196-8

Cengage Learning
200 First Stamford Place, 4th Floor
Stamford, CT 06902
USA

Cengage Learning is a leading provider of customized learning solutions with office locations around the globe, including Singapore, the United Kingdom, Australia, Mexico, Brazil, and Japan. Locate your local office at
www.cengage.com/global

Cengage Learning products are represented in Canada by Nelson Education, Ltd.

To learn more about Cengage Learning, visit **www.cengage.com**

Purchase any of our products at your local college store or at our preferred online store **www.cengagebrain.com**

Notice to the Reader

Publisher does not warrant or guarantee any of the products described herein or perform any independent analysis in connection with any of the product information contained herein. Publisher does not assume, and expressly disclaims, any obligation to obtain and include information other than that provided to it by the manufacturer. The reader is expressly warned to consider and adopt all safety precautions that might be indicated by the activities described herein and to avoid all potential hazards. By following the instructions contained herein, the reader willingly assumes all risks in connection with such instructions. The publisher makes no representations or warranties of any kind, including but not limited to, the warranties of fitness for particular purpose or merchantability, nor are any such representations implied with respect to the material set forth herein, and the publisher takes no responsibility with respect to such material. The publisher shall not be liable for any special, consequential, or exemplary damages resulting, in whole or part, from the readers' use of, or reliance upon, this material.

Printed in the United States of America
1 2 3 4 5 6 7 17 16 15 14 13

Table of Contents

Appendices

Preface

The transition from ICD-9-CM to ICD-10-CM/PCS will require extensive education and training for thousands of coding/billing professionals in the United States. This workbook is structured to provide hands-on application exercises for all specialty content areas of ICD-10-CM and a comprehensive, unique step-by-step approach for building a code in ICD-10-PCS.

The workbook was written for both the novice and experienced coder in any work setting. The new coder can use additional practice exercises to enhance his or her knowledge and skill in a variety of specialty areas of coding (ICD-10-CM or ICD-10-PCS) in order to continue to explore the characteristics of the classification systems. Many of the exercises were selected to emphasize key elements of ICD-10-CM/PCS and/or application of coding guidelines.

Assessment Methods

The variety of assessment techniques provides coders with methods to further identify their strengths and weaknesses in medical terminology, clinical concepts, and anatomy and physiology. With over 450 coding exercises/case studies and 50+ supplemental learning components, this workbook provides a wide-ranging tool for any coding training program. In addition to coding exercises, the supplemental assessments methods include:

- Matching Exercises
- Check Your Clinical Knowledge Completion Questions
- Identification of Anatomical Structures
- Applying Clinical Knowledge to Case Studies

Many of the distinctive characteristics of the workbook are outlined below:

Exercises

Each chapter has a variety of exercises that allow for a focused application of coding guidelines for that particular section. This chapter-by-chapter approach paves the way for "chunking" of content that can be easily referenced at a later date. The exercises highlight some of the most common diagnoses encountered in hospitals, physician offices, and alternative health care facilities.

New to This Edition

The workbook has been updated to include the latest ICD-10-CM and ICD-10-PCS code sets and guidelines. To allow users even more practice, each chapter now includes further coding assignments. In addition, the workbook contains more Operative Reports and decision tree examples for applying definitions of Root Operations. Chapter 20, "Coding with ICD-10-PCS," has also been expanded with exercises focusing on each individual character.

Transition from ICD-9-CM to ICD-10-CM

Students in education programs and experienced coders will be able to analyze the coding characteristics of ICD-9-CM compared to ICD-10-CM using a side-by-side approach in a chapter devoted to a compare-and-contrast activity. After implementation of ICD-10-CM/PCS, coders will still need to retrieve and analyze data from legacy systems that used ICD-9-CM. A total of 50 coding exercises allow for detailed examination of both systems.

Coding with ICD-10-PCS

The procedure coding system (PCS) chapter contains exercises highlighting several of the key elements for "building a code" using the new classification system. Emphasis will be placed on differentiating between root operations, body parts, approaches, devices, and qualifiers. Appendix C of the workbook provides a comprehensive list of the root operations and their definitions.

Application of Official Coding Guidelines

A key component before final selection of any code assignment is application of coding guidelines. Chapter 21 is dedicated to using case studies to emphasize the new ICD-10-CM/PCS *Official Guidelines for Coding and Reporting*.

Coding Case Studies

Chapter 22 permits coding professionals to integrate and apply all of their skills and knowledge to real-world case studies. The abstracts from health record documentation provide the entire story and permit a comprehensive review of the link between documentation and coding.

Computer-Assisted Coding

As technological systems become more advanced, computer-assisted coding will become a reality in the near future. Chapter 23 addresses the changes to workflow and abstracting key elements of documentation to support coding decisions. This last chapter permits coders to put all the pieces together to justify ICD-10-CM/PCS coding decisions in a simulated computer-assisted coding environment.

Detailed Answer Keys

All of the answers to the support questions (e.g., Check Your Clinical Knowledge) are provided in Appendix A of the workbook. In addition, answers to the first 5–10 coding exercises in each chapter are contained in Appendix A. At the request of faculty from training and education programs, the other half of the answers is only released to educators through online access to resources.

The majority of the chapters in the workbook provide detailed answer keys to assist coders with the methodology of using the Alphabetic Index, Table of Neoplasms, Table of Drugs and Chemicals, and the Tabular List.

Instructor Resources at the Instructor Companion Site

All instructor resources can be accessed at login.cengage.com to create a unique user login. Contact your sales representative for more information. Online instructor resources at the Instructor Companion site are password-protected and include the following:

- Complete answer key.

- Revisions to workbook due to coding changes as they become available.

ICD-10-CM/PCS Implementation Timeline

ICD-10-CM, including the *ICD-10-CM Official Guidelines for Coding and Reporting,* will replace the ICD-9-CM for all health care settings for diagnosis reporting with dates of service, or dates of discharge for inpatients, that occur on or after October 1, 2014. The Centers for Medicare & Medicaid Services (CMS) has stated that there will be no grace periods or delays.

ICD-10-PCS procedure codes will be required for hospital claims for inpatient hospital procedures only; however, facilities may elect to capture the codes for internal data analysis. ICD-10-PCS will not be used on physician claims, even those for inpatient visits. CPT and HCPCS will continue to be used for physician and ambulatory services including physician visits to inpatients. The following provides a visual snapshot of implementation dates by types of services:

October 1, 2014, Implementation Plan for Reporting Services

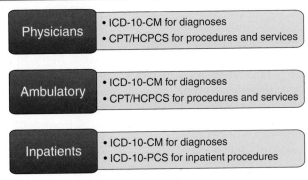

Bowman S, Brooks P. Preparing for ICD-10 Implementation in 2011 National Provider Teleconference

Annual updates for each system (ICD-10-CM and ICD-10-PCS) are posted on the CMS website.

Partial Code Freeze

The annual updates to the coding systems make transition planning difficult for vendors, system administrators, third-party payers, and educators who must prepare in advance of the October 1, 2014, implementation date. For that reason, CMS has published the following schedule for freezing the code sets:

Date	Freeze Initiative
October 1, 2011	Last regular annual updates to both ICD-9-CM and ICD-10-CM
October 1, 2012	Limited code updates to both ICD-9-CM and ICD-10-CM code sets. Updates will be only focused on new technology and new diseases.
October 1, 2013	Limited code updates to ICD-10-CM to capture new technology and new diseases.
October 1, 2013– October 1, 2014	No updates for ICD-9-CM
October 1, 2015	Regular updates to ICD-10-CM will begin

Education and Training

Experts suggest that *intensive* coder training should be conducted 6 to 9 months prior to implementation. For experienced coders, a 2-day training session will likely be sufficient.

About the Authors

Mary Jo Bowie, MS, BS, AAS, RHIA, RHIT

Mary Jo has worked in the health information field for over 30 years as a consultant, HIM director, and college instructor. She is owner of Health Information Professional Services in Binghamton, New York, and an instructor, in the health information technology program, at Broome Community College, Binghamton, New York. Mary Jo is an active member of the American Health Information Management Association. She has served the New York State Health Information Management Association as education director and on the board of directors, 1989–1991; Ambulatory Care Coding Guidelines (ACGC) Committee, 1995–2001; and chairperson, ACGC Committee, 1993–1995. She was the American Health Information Management Association nominee for New York State for National Award for Literary Contribution to Profession, 1993 and 1994. At the collegiate level, teaching both in the classroom and in an Internet-based format, she has taught numerous health information technology and coding and reimbursement classes. Mary Jo has conducted professional coding workshops for coders as well as for physicians and clinical staff. Mary Jo is a coding trainer for the Cengage TEAM UP program that offers professional workshops to college faculty. She has conducted numerous workshops on ICD-10-CM and ICD-10-PCS. Ms. Bowie has completed the AHIMA train the trainer program for ICD-10-CM/PCS from AHIMA.

Gail Smith, MA, RHIA, CCS-P

Gail I. Smith is president of Gail I. Smith Consulting, LLC in Cincinnati, Ohio. Prior to starting a consulting business in 2011, Gail was an associate professor and director of the Health Information Management (HIM) program at the University of Cincinnati. Previously, she served as the director of the HIM program at Cincinnati State Technical and Community College for 18 years. Before a career in education, Smith held management positions in two Cincinnati hospitals. On a part-time basis, Gail has served as a coding consultant for over 30 years. Her projects include developing content for courses/workshops, delivering seminars, performing coding reviews, and mapping ICD-10-CM/PCS for database conversions. Ms. Smith is an AHIMA-approved ICD-10-CM/PCS Trainer and a member of the AHIMA Academy Faculty.

Ms. Smith has authored several coding textbooks and is a national speaker and content expert on e-Learning and instructional design.

Gail has served as president of the Ohio Health Information Management Association and received the Professional Achievement Award in 1996 and Distinguished Member Award in 2005. Gail also served on the Board of Directors of the American Health Information Management Association from 2003 through 2006.

Ms. Smith received her bachelor's degree in HIM from The Ohio State University and her master's degree in education from the College of Mt. St. Joseph in Cincinnati, Ohio.

Acknowledgements

To my husband, Bill, who always supports me in all of my writing projects and everything I have done for the last 30 years. To my daughters, Sarah and Bethannie, and my parents, who encourage me to keep on going.

To the Cengage family, especially Rhonda Dearborn and Lauren Whalen, who guided the creation of the book.

To my technical reviewer, Patricia Griffin for her attention to detail and commitment to the project. You are a joy to work with!

—Mary Jo Bowie

To my technical reviewer, Lynn Kuehn, for her attention to detail.

I wish to acknowledge my husband, Mark, and daughter, Kristin, for their endless support and encouraging words.

—Gail Smith

Technical Reviewers

Patricia Griffin, RHIT
Health Information Consultant/Instructor
Binghamton, NY

Lynn Kuehn, MS, RHIA, CCS-P, FAHIMA
President
Kuehn Consulting, LLC
Waukesha, WI

Reviewers

Rhoda Cooper, CPC, RMC, NCICS
Director of HIM
Piedmont Virginia Community College
Charlottesville, VA

Robin Douglas
Medical Office/Billing & Coding Instructor
Holmes Community College
Grenada, MS

Rashmi Gaonkar, MS, MHA (Inf)
Senior Instructor/ Subject Specialist
ASA College
Brooklyn, NY

Carrie Heinz, RHIT
Health Information Management Director
Rolette Community Care Center
Rolette, ND

Barbara Marchelletta
Allied Health Program Director
Beal College
Bangor, ME

Susan Walther, RHIA, CCS
HIM Department Head
Greenville Technical College
Greenville, SC

21. Legionnaires' disease _____

22. Early congenital syphilitic pneumonia _____

23. Ringworm of nails, right hand _____

24. Tuberculous pneumothorax _____

25. Mumps complicated by hepatitis _____

26. Clostridial cellulitis _____

27. Chlamydial peritionitis _____

28. Enteroviral encephalomyelitis _____

29. Acute gastroenteropathy due to small round virus _____

30. Ross River fever _____

31. Cutaneous larva migrans _____

32. Hepatitis A with hepatic coma _____

33. Ocular myiasis _____

34. Kaposi's varicelliform eruption _____

35. Syphilitic chancre _____

2

Neoplasms

The chapter on neoplasms contains codes for most benign and malignant neoplasms; however, certain benign neoplasms may be found in the other chapters. Coders must identify the morphology (behavior) of the neoplasm to appropriately classify as benign, in situ, malignant, or of uncertain behavior. The ICD-10-CM Neoplasm Table is located after the Alphabetic Index. Codes that appear with a dash (–) at the end (e.g., Neoplasm, auditory canal C44.2–) require verification in the Tabular List to complete the code assignment.

Check Your Knowledge of Neoplasms

Identify the following neoplasms as "B" for benign, "M" for malignant, or "U" for uncertain behavior. Locating the morphological term in the Alphabetic Index will assist with this exercise. Answers are located in Appendix A.

_____ **1.** Adenoma of prostate

_____ **2.** Infiltrating duct carcinoma of the breast

_____ **3.** Osteofibroma of the femur

_____ **4.** Endometrioid adenoma (pathology report states borderline malignancy)

_____ **5.** Hepatic mesenchymal sarcoma

Check Your Clinical Knowledge

Circle one of the selections provided in parentheses to complete the following sentences. Answers are located in Appendix A.

1. The pathology report states that the patient has carcinoma in situ of the cervix. This morphology indicates that the cancer cells have _____. (spread beyond the borders, not invaded the surrounding tissues)

2. _____ is most often identified as skin cancer. (Melanoma, Mesothelioma)

3. A uterine leiomyoma is commonly known as a _____. (fibroid, cystic lesion)

4. Condylomas are commonly known as _____. (plantar warts, genital warts)

5. An adenomatous polyp in the colon would be identified as a _____ tumor. (benign, malignant)

Coding

Assign ICD-10-CM codes to the following. Answers to exercises 1–10 are located in Appendix A, and the remaining answers are provided only to educators through the instructor online companion.

1. Myxofibrosarcoma of the neck _____

2. Female patient was diagnosed with carcinoma of the lower-inner quadrant of the right breast _____

3. Malignant melanoma of the skin of the cheek _____

4. Carcinoma of the upper lobe of the right lung with metastasis to the bone (spinal column) _____

5. Adenocarcinoma of the prostate _____

6. Osteofibroma of the right femur _____

7. Condyloma acuminatum of the penis _____

8. Diffuse lymphoblastic lymphoma (of lymph nodes of left axilla and arm) _____

9. Mixed glioma of the right optic nerve _____

10. Malignant melanoma of forehead _____

11. Benign adenomatous polyp of the descending colon _____

12. Osteoblastoma of the left thumb _____

13. Carcinoma of the anterior wall of the bladder _____

14. Wilms tumor, left kidney _____

15. Carcinoma of the colon with metastasis to the liver and lung (middle lobe) _____

16. Merkel cell carcinoma of the nose _____

17. Pleural mesothelioma, malignant _____

18. Basal cell carcinoma of the left pinna   _____

19. Adenocarcinoma of the larynx (cancerous lesion
overlapping several sites in the larynx)   _____

20. Transitional cell papilloma of the bladder   _____

21. Adenomatosis, pulmonary   _____

22. Granulocytic leukemia in remission   _____

23. Carcinoma in situ of colon   _____

24. Neoplasm of lingual tonsil, benign   _____

25. Melanocytic nevi of anal skin   _____

26. Malignant neoplasm of adenoid, primary   _____

27. Alpha heavy chain disease   _____

28. Multiple myeloma in remission   _____

29. Invasive hydatidiform mole   _____

30. Neoplasm of uncertain behavior of left breast   _____

Diseases of the Blood and Blood-Forming Organs

This short chapter includes blocks of codes for reporting anemia and other disorders of blood and blood-forming organs. Coders are cautioned to read notes that provide guidance for "code first," "code also," and "use additional code" for this chapter.

Example: D61.82 Myelophthisis

Code also the underlying disorder, such as:
malignant neoplasm of breast (C50.-)
tuberculosis (A15.-)

Check Your Clinical Knowledge

Match the following clinical description with the diagnosis that would best support the findings. Answers are located in Appendix A.

Clinical Description

1. _____ 34-year-old man experiences excessive bleeding after surgery, reports that he bruised easily.

2. _____ 5-year-old African American child reports abdominal pain and trouble breathing. Clinician notes delayed growth.

3. _____ 22-year-old woman, who is a vegetarian, reports chronic fatigue, generalized aching, and insomnia.

4. _____ 5-year-old child is pale, tired, and irritable. Recently treated for digestive disorder. Reddish tint to urine.

5. _____ Child experiences excessive bleeding following circumcision. Lab results reveal hereditary clotting disorder.

Diagnosis

a. sickle cell disease

b. vitamin B deficiency

c. von Willebrand disease

d. Christmas disease (hemophilia B)

e. hemolytic uremic syndrome

Coding

Assign ICD-10-CM codes to the following. Answers to exercises 1–5 are located in Appendix A, and the remaining answers are provided only to educators through the instructor online companion.

1. Posttraumatic cyst of the spleen   _____

2. Christmas disease (hemophilia B)   _____

3. Normocytic chronic blood loss anemia   _____

4. Vitamin B12 deficiency anemia—vegan anemia   _____

5. Coagulation disorder, factor X   _____

6. Alpha thalassemia trait   _____

7. Congenital neutropenia with fever   _____

8. Abnormal hemoglobin   _____

9. Sickle cell anemia, Hb-SE with crisis and acute chest syndrome   _____

10. von Willebrand disease   _____

11. Iron deficiency anemia   _____

12. G6PD deficiency anemia   _____

13. Hemophilia A   _____

14. Vascular purpura   _____

15. Basophilic leukopenia   _____

16. Nutritional megaloblastic anemia   _____

17. Secondary hemophilia   _____

18. Hereditary thromboasthenia   _____

19. Infantile genetic agranulocytosis   _____

20. Essential cryoglobulinemia   _____

Endocrine, Nutritional, and Metabolic Diseases

This chapter is dominated by codes for diseases associated with diabetes mellitus. The combination codes identify the type of diabetes, the body system affected, and the complications affecting that body system.

> Example: E10.331 Type 1 diabetes mellitus with moderate nonproliferative diabetic retinopathy with macular edema

Even though the combination codes thoroughly describe the conditions, occasionally a note will appear that instructs the coder to use an additional code (e.g., use *additional code to identify the stage of chronic kidney disease*) or "code first" such as in the following example.

> Example: E66.1 Drug-induced obesity
> Code first (T36-T50) to identify the drug

Check Your Clinical Knowledge: Case Studies

Match the following clinical descriptions in the case studies with the diagnosis that would best support the findings. Answers are located in Appendix A.

Case Study #1

HISTORY: This 52-year-old man complains of polyuria and polydipsia. He reports that he has gained weight over the years but more recently has been losing weight even though his appetite is the same.

PHYSICAL EXAMINATION: Hypertensive male (BP 180/90) who is obese.

LABORATORY FINDINGS: Fasting plasma glucose 168 mg/dL. Urinalysis: protein and glucose present.

DISEASE MANAGEMENT: Nutritionist will discuss lifestyle changes and dietary modification program. Glucotrol prescribed.

This profile would best support which of the following diagnoses? _____

a. Type 1 diabetes mellitus

b. Type 2 diabetes mellitus

c. Graves disease

d. Hypothyroidism

Case Study #2

HISTORY: A 35-year-old woman reports palpitations, frequent bouts of anxiety, profuse sweating, and the inability to concentrate for the past couple of months.

PHYSICAL EXAMINATION: Low-grade fever with tachycardia. Thyroid gland is enlarged without tenderness. Papules noted over the shins.

LABORATORY FINDINGS: Mild leukocytosis with normal glucose. TSH: High.

IMAGING: Nuclear thyroid scan revealed diffuse uptake throughout the thyroid gland.

DISEASE MANAGEMENT: Propranolol for treatment of rapid heart rate and anxiety. Tapazole prescribed, twice daily.

This profile would best support which of the following diagnoses? _____

a. Type 1 diabetes mellitus

b. Type 2 diabetes mellitus

c. Graves disease

d. Hypothyroidism

Case Study #3

HISTORY: This 19-year-old woman reports that she has been feeling tired and has excessive thirst and recent weight loss over the past several weeks.

PHYSICAL EXAMINATION: Vital signs: No fever; normal blood pressure, elevated R/R. Thin, lethargic female with poor skin turgor and fruity smell on breath.

LABORATORY FINDINGS: Hyponatremia, decreased bicarbonate, elevated glucose, and ketonuria.

DISEASE MANAGEMENT: IV insulin, hydration, and correction of electrolyte imbalance. Treatment will include dietary education and regular glucose monitoring and periodic glycosylated hemoglobin (HbA1c).

This profile would best support which of the following diagnoses? _____

a. Type 1 diabetes mellitus

b. Type 2 diabetes mellitus

c. Graves disease

d. Hypothyroidism

Case Study #4

Patient is a 58-year-old woman with Type 1 diabetes and peripheral neuropathy disease. Over the past 20 months, she has developed a (diabetic) skin ulcer of the left ankle. This type of skin ulcer would be classified as a: _____.

a. Decubitus

b. Pressure ulcer

c. Nonpressure ulcer

Coding

Assign ICD-10-CM codes to the following. Answers to exercises 1–5 are located in Appendix A, and the remaining answers are provided only to educators through the instructor online companion.

1. Graves disease   _____

2. Hyperkalemia   _____

3. Vitamin B12 deficiency   _____

4. Diabetic cataract, Type 1 diabetic patient   _____

5. Type 1 diabetes with diabetic chronic skin ulcer of the left
heel and midfoot (*breakdown of skin only*)   _____

6. Idiopathic hypoparathyroidism   _____

7. Type 1 diabetes mellitus with chronic stage III kidney disease
as a result of the diabetes   _____

8. Hypocalcemia   _____

9. Elevated triglycerides and cholesterol levels   _____

10. Type 2 diabetes mellitus with proliferative diabetic retinopathy
with macular edema   _____

11. Infarction of thyroid   _____

12. Deficiency of Vitamin C   _____

13. Dysfunction of pineal gland   _____

14. Postirradiation hypopituitarism   _____

15. Respiratory acidosis   _____

Mental, Behavioral, and Neurodevelopmental Disorders

This section was developed alongside the American Psychiatric Association's *Diagnostic & Statistical Manual of Mental Disorders* (DSM), which provides a common language and standard criteria for the classification of mental disorders in the United States. Although the coding system in *DSM* is designed to correspond with ICD, there are some differences. The two publications are not revised on the same schedule. The fifth edition of *DSM* is scheduled for publication in May 2013.

Check Your Clinical Knowledge

Match the following clinical description with the diagnosis that would best support the findings. Answers are located in Appendix A.

Clinical Description

1. _____ inattentive, impulsive, and hyperactive

2. _____ loss of interest, no pleasure in life

3. _____ episodes of palpitations, diaphoresis, fear of losing control

4. _____ flashbacks, nightmares, intrusive memories

5. _____ delusional, hallucinations, disorganized thinking

Diagnosis

a. panic disorder

b. schizophrenia

c. depression

d. attention-deficit disorder

e. posttraumatic stress syndrome

Coding

Assign ICD-10-CM codes to the following. Answers to exercises 1–5 are located in Appendix A, and the remaining answers are provided only to educators through the instructor online companion.

1. Anorexia nervosa—patient alternates between binge eating and purging _____

2. Posttraumatic stress disorder, acute _____

3. Complete auditory hallucinations _____

4. Bipolar disorder (current episode of depression), mild   _____

5. Schizotypal personality disorder   _____

6. Chronic alcoholism, dependence with intoxication   _____

7. Early onset of Alzheimer disease with aggressive, combative behavior   _____

8. Alcohol abuse, patient is intoxicated   _____

9. Cocaine dependence, cocaine-induced anxiety disorder   _____

10. Manic-depressive disorder, recurrent, mild   _____

11. Depressive neurosis   _____

12. Fear of blood   _____

13. Anxiety hysteria   _____

14. Dissociative convulsions   _____

15. Psychogenic teeth grinding   _____

16. Depressive personality disorder   _____

17. Psychasthenic neurosis   _____

18. Pica in an adult   _____

19. IQ of 25   _____

20. Abuse of vitamins   _____

Diseases of Nervous System (Eyes and Ears)

This chapter focuses on coding diseases of the nervous system as well as the eye/adnexa and ear and mastoid process. Neurologic diseases are disorders of the brain, spinal cord, and nerves throughout the body. Referencing the Tabular List of ICD-10-CM, this chapter of this workbook encompasses Chapters 6, 7, and 8 of ICD-10-CM. Exercises in this chapter will include common diseases from the following categories of codes:

> G codes   – Diseases of Nervous System
> H codes (H00-H59) – Disorders of the Eye and Adnexa
> H codes (H60-H95) – Diseases of the Ear and Mastoid Process

Check Your Clinical Knowledge

Circle one of the selections provided in parentheses to complete the following sentences. Answers are located in Appendix A.

1. The physician documents that the patient's middle ear infection was producing pus. Producing pus would be classified as _____. (exostosis, purulent)

2. The elderly patient's eyelids were drooping and causing problems with vision. The physician scheduled the patient for surgery with the diagnosis of _____. (dermatochalasis, dermatitis)

3. The physician noted that the patient's _____ pain was severe, constant, and not curable. (chronic, intractable)

4. The documentation states that the patient's eye (iris and ciliary body) is swollen and inflamed. The physician concludes with the diagnosis of _____. (iridocyclitis, synechiae)

5. The pathology report describes the _____ as a noncancerous growth of the conjunctiva. (presbyopia, pterygium)

● Coding

Assign ICD-10-CM codes to the following. Answers to exercises 1–10 are located in Appendix A, and the remaining answers are provided only to educators through the instructor online companion.

1. Left ulnar nerve entrapment at the elbow   _____

2. Left tympanic membrane perforation   _____

3. Intracranial meningioma   _____

4. Retinal detachment, left eye   _____

5. Carpal tunnel compression, left, severe   _____

6. Patient seen in emergency department as a result of an injury at work. Diagnosis: Foreign body of left eye—sliver of metal located in cornea   _____

7. Dermatochalasis of bilateral upper eyelids   _____

8. Acute otitis media, left, producing pus   _____

9. Classic migraine, intractable with aura   _____

10. Spastic hemiplegia of right (dominant) side   _____

11. Recurrent, acute iridocyclitis of both eyes   _____

12. Meningoencephalitis   _____

13. Recurrent pterygium, right eye   _____

14. Intraspinal extradural abscess   _____

15. Nasolacrimal duct obstruction due to stenosis, right eye   _____

16. Multiple perforations of tympanic membrane of both left and right ears   _____

17. Conductive hearing loss, right ear   _____

18. Episodic, tension headaches   _____

19. Streptococcal group A meningitis   _____

20. Macular hole, right eye   _____

21. Bilateral, hyphema   _____

22. Retinal hemorrhage of the right eye   _____

23. Abscess of the left external ear   _____

24. Ototoxic hearing loss   _____

25. Acute mastoiditis of the left ear   _____

26. Motor neuron disease   _____

27. Mesial temporal sclerosis   _____

28. Cochlear otosclerosis, both ears   _____

29. Acoustic trauma of inner right ear   _____

30. Cellulitis of left external ear   _____

Diseases of the Circulatory System

The chapter on diseases of the circulatory system can be challenging because of the anatomy, the complexity of the guidelines, and the detailed documentation necessary for an accurate code assignment. A significant change between ICD-9-CM and ICD-10-CM occurred with the definition of acute myocardial infarction (AMI). In ICD-10-CM guidelines, an acute AMI is described as being 4 weeks or less in contrast to 8 weeks in ICD-9-CM.

Check Your Knowledge of Anatomy

Label Figure 7-1 correctly by using the following terms. Answers are located in Appendix A.

Aortic valve

Mitral valve

Pulmonic valve

Tricuspid valve

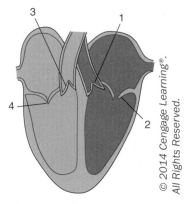

© 2014 Cengage Learning®. All Rights Reserved.

Figure 7-1

Check Your Clinical Knowledge

Circle one of the selections provided in parentheses to complete the following sentences. Answers are located in Appendix A.

1. The patient's blood pressure is 150/85. The number 85 is referred to as the _____ pressure. (diastolic, systolic)

2. A(n) _____ is a blood clot that forms in the vessel and *does not* move to another area of the body. (embolus, thrombus)

3. As a result of a stroke, the patient has difficulty swallowing and is ordered therapy for treatment of _____. (dysphagia, dysphasia)

4. The documentation in the health records indicates that the patient has a rapid heart rate, which supports the diagnosis of _____. (brachycardia, tachycardia)

5. The surgeon documented that the _____ artery in the neck was occluded and caused the stroke. (carotid, coronary)

Coding

Assign ICD-10-CM codes to the following. Answers to exercises 1–10 are located in Appendix A, and the remaining answers are provided only to educators through the instructor online companion.

1. Acute, diastolic congestive heart failure _____

2. Rheumatic aortic valve stenosis _____

3. Pulmonary embolism with acute cor pulmonale _____

4. Acute posterolateral-transmural myocardial infarction (ST elevation [STEMI]) _____

5. Hypertensive heart disease with chronic (systolic and diastolic) heart failure _____

6. Cerebrovascular accident due to thrombosis of left vertebral artery _____

7. Premature ventricular contractions _____

8. Cerebrovascular infarction due to embolism of right middle cerebral artery _____

9. Left bundle branch block _____

10. Patient treated in the outpatient clinic for dysphagia (pharyngeal phase) as a residual from a previous intracerebral hemorrhage _____

11. Chronic aortic regurgitation _____

12. Patent ductus arteriosus _____

13. Mitral valve prolapse syndrome _____

14. Hypertensive heart disease with chronic stage 5 kidney disease _____

15. Atrial paroxysmal tachycardia _____

16. Residual hemiplegia, left nondominant side (patient suffered cerebral infarction several months earlier) _____

17. Three weeks after sustaining an STEMI of the inferior wall, the patient is seen in the physician's office for a follow-up appointment _____

18. Patient currently treated as an inpatient for acute cerebrovascular infarction (thrombosis of left cerebellar artery) with resulting hemiplegia on the right dominant side _____

19. Acute bacterial (*Staphylococcus aureus*) endocarditis _____

20. Arteriosclerotic heart disease (ASHD) with angina; no history of bypass surgery _____

21. Healed MI _____

22. Silent myocardial ischemia _____

23. Chronic cor pulmonale _____

24. Giant cell myocarditis _____

25. Sinoatrial block _____

26. Chronic rheumatic myopericarditis _____

27. Occlusion and stenosis of right carotid artery _____

28. Congenital cardiomyopathy _____

29. Cardiac hypertrophy _____

30. SA block _____

Diseases of the Respiratory System

The respiratory system contains many combination codes because related conditions overlap in the disease process. The following are some of the unique characteristics of coding in this chapter.

Example 1

Disease	With Chronic Bronchitis	Without Chronic Bronchitis
Emphysema	J44.- Other chronic obstructive pulmonary disease	J43.- Emphysema

Example 2

Disease	With Chronic Obstructive Pulmonary Disease	Without Chronic Obstructive Pulmonary Disease
Asthma	J44.- Other chronic obstructive pulmonary disease *Coders are instructed to also code the type of asthma (J45.-) if applicable*	J45.- Asthma

Check Your Knowledge of Anatomy

Label Figure 8-1 correctly by using the following terms. Answers are located in Appendix A.

Alveoli

Bronchiole

Bronchus

Larynx

Mouth

Nasal cavity

Pharynx

Right lung

Trachea

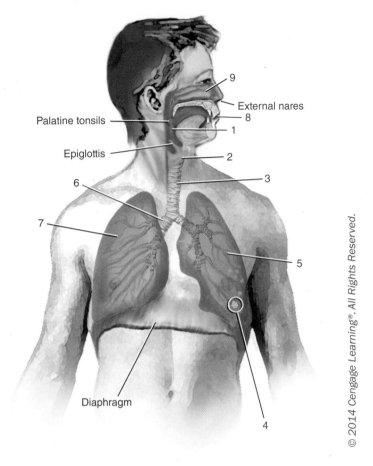

Figure 8-1

Check Your Clinical Knowledge

Circle one of the selections provided in parentheses to complete the following sentences. Answers are located in Appendix A.

1. The patient has a piece of candy stuck in his throat that is causing irritation. The physician documents examination of the _____. (pharynx, larynx)

2. The physician documents that the patient has a buildup of fluid in the air sacs of the lungs. This documentation supports the diagnosis of _____. (pneumothorax, pulmonary edema)

3. The physician documents that the patient has wheezing, shortness of breath, and chest tightness. It was noted that the family recently adopted a cat. The documentation supports the diagnosis of _____. (asthma, bronchitis)

4. The physician notes that there is swelling and mucus buildup in the smallest air passages in the lungs, or the _____. (bronchioles, pleura)

5. The physician documents that the patient has a bacterial pneumonia. The laboratory test revealed _____ as the organism. (histoplasmosis, *Pseudomonas*)

Coding

Assign ICD-10-CM codes to the following. Answers to exercises 1–10 are located in Appendix A, and the remaining answers are provided only to educators through the instructor online companion.

1. Hypertrophic adenoids and tonsils

2. Chronic pulmonary edema

3. Obstructive rhinitis

4. Chronic obstructive pulmonary disease (COPD) with acute bronchitis

5. Bilateral, complete cleft palate with cleft lip

6. Maxillary nasal polyp

7. Severe, persistent asthma with acute exacerbation

8. Bronchopneumonia due to *staphylococci*

9. Acute pharyngitis due to influenza

10. A 6-year-old child is seen for acute respiratory distress syndrome

11. Asthmatic bronchitis

12. Patient presents with cough, fever, and a stuffy nose. Diagnosis: Influenza due to novel influenza A virus

13. Acute laryngitis

14. Chronic obstructive asthma with acute exacerbation

15. Acute bronchitis with bronchiectasis

16. COPD with chronic bronchitis and pulmonary emphysema

17. Acute bronchiolitis with bronchospasm

18. Acute and chronic respiratory failure

19. The surgeon documents that the patient is experiencing acute pulmonary insufficiency immediately following a partial lobectomy

20. Patient seen in the emergency department for a piece of chicken bone
lodged in pharynx that is causing discomfort and scraping   _____

21. Chronic tonsillitis and adenoiditis   _____

22. Bilateral paralysis of glottis   _____

23. Edema of pharynx   _____

24. Coalworker's lung disease   _____

25. Pulmonary alveolar proteinosis   _____

26. Acute recurrent frontal sinusitis   _____

27. Acute bronchitis due to rhinovirus   _____

28. Chronic tonsillitis and adenoiditis   _____

29. Edema of glottis   _____

30. Leukoplakia of vocal cords   _____

Diseases of the Digestive System

As with other chapters within ICD-10-CM, the chapter for the digestive system also contains many combination codes. Many coding assignments depend on documentation to identify whether bleeding, perforation, gangrene, or another condition complicated the diagnosis. Note the following examples that depict the detailed diagnostic information within the code selections:

Code Category	**With** presence of complication(s)	**Without** presence of complication(s)
K57 Diverticular disease of intestine	K57.01 Diverticulitis of small intestine *with* perforation and abscess with bleeding	K57.12 Diverticulitis of small intestine *without* perforation or abscess without bleeding
K51.5 Left-sided colitis	K51.511 Left-sided colitis *with* rectal bleeding K51.512 Left-sided colitis *with* intestinal obstruction	K51.50 Left-sided colitis *without* complications
K43 Ventral hernia	K43.11 Incisional hernia *with* gangrene K43.19 Other ventral hernia, *with* gangrene	K43.91 Incisional hernia, *without* obstruction or gangrene

Check Your Knowledge of Anatomy

Label Figure 9-1 correctly by using the following terms. Answers are located in Appendix A.

Esophagus	Ascending colon
Duodenum	Oral cavity
Appendix	Ileum
Pharynx	Anus
Rectum	Sigmoid colon
Jejunum	Descending colon

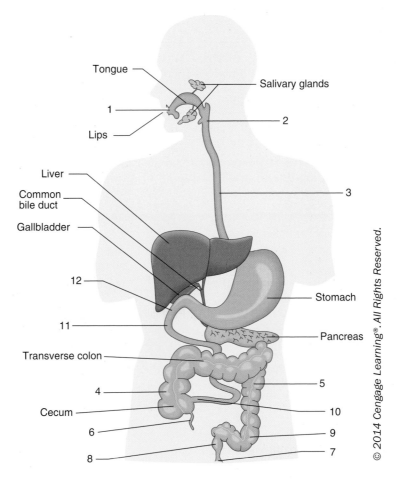

Figure 9-1

Check Your Clinical Knowledge

Circle one of the selections provided in parentheses to complete the following sentences. Answers are located in Appendix A.

1. The surgeon noted that stones were located in the bile duct and documented the diagnosis of _____. (cholelithiasis, choledocholithiasis)

2. The operative report explained that an excessive amount of fluid was located in the peritoneal cavity. This statement was consistent with the postoperative diagnosis of _____. (ascites, varices)

3. The pathology report revealed that the gallbladder was inflamed, which supported the postoperative diagnosis of _____. (cholecystitis, cholangitis)

4. The physical examination revealed a protrusion of the intestine through a weakening of the abdominal wall near the groin. This finding supports the diagnosis of a _____ hernia. (hiatal, femoral)

5. The operative report revealed a stricture in the small intestine, supporting documentation of a narrowing of the _____. (rectum, ileum)

Coding

Assign ICD-10-CM codes to the following. Answers to exercises 1–10 are located in Appendix A, and the remaining answers are provided only to educators through the instructor online companion.

1. Recurrent distal esophageal stricture   _____

2. Chronic hepatic failure   _____

3. Gastrointestinal bleeding due to angiodysplasia of stomach and duodenum   _____

4. Alcoholic hepatitis with ascites   _____

5. Perforated acute duodenal ulcer   _____

6. Preoperative diagnosis: Polyp of the colon. Pathology report states adenocarcinoma of the ascending colon   _____

7. Diverticulosis of ileum with hemorrhaging   _____

8. External hemorrhoids   _____

9. Acute gastritis with hemorrhaging   _____

10. Ulcerated esophageal varices   _____

11. Choledocholithiasis with acute cholecystitis   _____

12. Paraesophageal hernia   _____

13. Acute appendicitis with subsequent rupture and widespread peritonitis   _____

14. Chronic peptic ulcer with both hemorrhage and perforation   _____

15. Diverticulitis of duodenum   _____

16. Acute gingivitis   _____

17. Gastroesophageal reflux disease (GERD)   _____

18. Irritable bowel syndrome with frequent bouts of diarrhea   _____

19. Left-strangulated femoral hernia causing obstruction   _____

20. Crohn's disease of ileum with abscess   _____

21. Sciatic hernia   _____

22. Ulcerative proctitis with fistula   _____

23. Left-sided colitis   _____

24. Acute intestinal infarction   _____

25. Paralysis of bowel   _____

26. Generalized gingival recession   _____

27. Acute duodenal ulcer with perforation   _____

28. Abscess of esophagus   _____

29. Chronic atrophic gastritis with bleeding   _____

30. Nontraumatic tear of anus   _____

CHAPTER 10

Diseases of the Skin and Subcutaneous Tissue

This chapter of ICD-10-CM contains codes that report various diseases of the skin and subcutaneous tissue with great specificity at the fourth and fifth character levels. Instructional notations are used to instruct the coder to:

- Code first any associated condition
- Code first underlying disease
- Use additional code to identify organism
- Code first (T36-T65) to identify drug or substance

Check Your Knowledge of Anatomy

Label Figure 10-1 correctly by using the following terms. Answers are located in Appendix A.

Arrector pili muscle

Dermis

Epidermis

Hair follicle

Hair shaft

Papilla of hair

Sebaceous (oil) gland

Sweat gland

Sweat pore

Subcutaneous fatty tissue

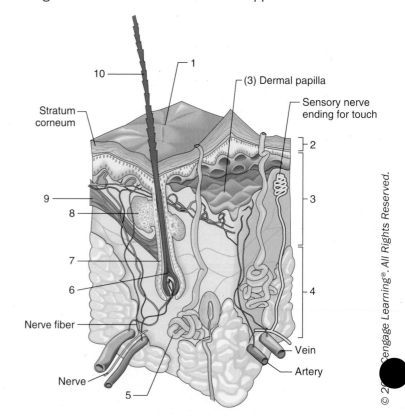

Figure 10-1

Check Your Clinical Knowledge

Circle one of the selections provided in parentheses to complete the following sentences. Answers are located in Appendix A.

1. _____ is an extremely contagious skin disease that most commonly affects the face and hands and is caused by *Streptococcus* and staphylococcal bacteria. (Plantar warts, Impetigo)

2. _____, a noncontagious chronic skin disease, is characterized by a rapid replacement of epidermal cells that appears as red raised lesions with silvery colored scales. (Psoriasis, Candidiasis)

3. Skin redness, also known as _____, is a common sign that occurs for many conditions of the integumentary system. (hematoma, erythema)

4. Erosion of the skin or mucous membrane that results in tissue loss due to prolonged pressure on the affected area is known as a pressure ulcer or a _____ ulcer. (decubitus, papule)

5. A boil, also known as a _____, is a small abscess that occurs in the tissues of the skin generally around a hair follicle. (furuncle, carbuncle)

Coding

Assign ICD-10-CM codes to the following. Answers to exercises 1–10 are located in Appendix A, and the remaining answers are provided only to educators through the instructor online companion.

1. Acute lymphadenitis of axilla _____

2. Circumscribed neurodermatitis _____

3. Yellow nail syndrome _____

4. Urticaria due to cold _____

5. Acute lymphangitis of left arm _____

6. Dry skin dermatitis _____

7. Pressure sore of elbow, stage I _____

8. Pilonidal cyst with abscess _____

9. Allergic dermatitis due to contact with chromium, initial visit _____

10. Androgenic alopecia _____

11. Postprocedural hematoma of skin following a dermatologic procedure _____

12. Acne necrotica miliaris _____

13. Chronic infantile eczema _____⬤

14. Infectious eczematoid dermatitis _____

15. Psoriatic arthritis mutilans _____

16. Sixth visit to treat chronic radiodermatitis due to exposure to laser radiation _____

17. Dermatosis papulosa nigra _____

18. Stage IV pressure ulcer of tailbone area with gangrene _____

19. Third-degree sunburn _____

20. Primary focal hyperhidrosis on palms of hands _____

21. Impetigo neonatorum _____

22. Recurrent periodic urticaria _____

23. Nail dystrophy _____⬤

24. Psoriasis, arthropathic _____

25. Retiformis parapsoriasis _____

26. Pilondial cyst with abscess _____

27. Furuncle of right foot _____

28. Small plaque parapsoriasis _____

29. Solar keratosis _____

30. Perforating granuloma annulare _____

Diseases of the Musculoskeletal System and Connective Tissue

Laterality and anatomical specificity are used for many of the codes that report diseases of the musculoskeletal system and connective tissue. Seventh-character extensions are used to provide additional information. Instructional notations are used to alert coders to add additional codes and the notations of "Code first..." denote code sequencing.

Check Your Knowledge of Anatomy and Disorders

Label the figures correctly by using the following terms. Answers are located in Appendix A.

A. Terms for Figures 11-1, 11-2, and 11-3

Kyphosis

Lordosis

Scoliosis

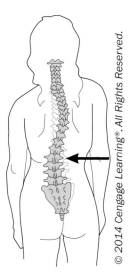

Figure 11-1

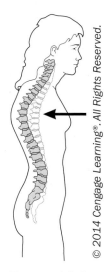

Figure 11-2

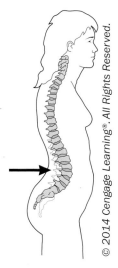

Figure 11-3

B. Terms for Figure 11-4

Cervical vertebrae   Sacrum

Coccyx   Thoracic (dorsal) vertebrae

Intervertebral disc   Vertebral body

Lumbar vertebrae

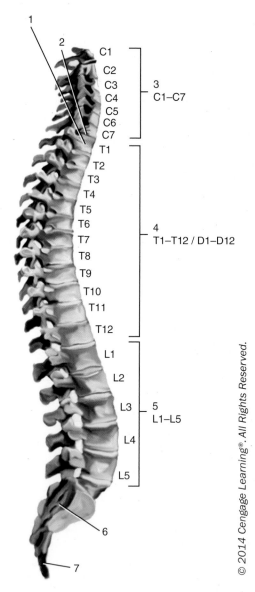

Figure 11-4

Check Your Clinical Knowledge

Circle one of the selections provided in parentheses to complete the following sentences. Answers are located in Appendix A.

1. _____ is a metabolic disease that causes the bone to have a Swiss cheese–like appearance that leads to bone mass loss. (Arthritis, Osteoporosis)

2. The term "bunion" is commonly used for _____, a deformity that affects the metatarsophalangeal joint of the big toe. (hallux valgus, rheumatoid arthritis)

3. The physician documents the following: "In the patient's right hand there is fusion and total loss of joint function." This would suggest that the patient has _____ of the hand. (ankylosis, bursitis)

4. _____ is caused by a deficiency of vitamin D and results in the softening of the bones. (Osteomalacia, Osteomyelitis)

5. A(n) _____ is used to evaluate muscle disorders by inserting a small needle into the muscle tissue and recording the electrical activity. (dual-energy X-ray absorptiometry scan, electromyography)

Coding

Assign ICD-10-CM codes to the following. Answers to exercises 1–10 are located in Appendix A, and the remaining answers are provided only to educators through the instructor online companion.

1. Juvenile osteochondrosis of pelvis   _____

2. Rheumatoid vasculitis with rheumatoid arthritis of left shoulder   _____

3. Rheumatoid bursitis of the right foot and ankle   _____

4. Acute gout flare   _____

5. Left foot, acquired hallux rigidus   _____

6. Acquired clubfoot of right foot   _____

7. Recurrent subluxation of patella, left knee   _____

8. Loose body in third left toe joint   _____

9. Myositis ossificans progressiva, left upper arm   _____

10. Right hip abscess of bursa caused by *Staphylococcus aureus*   _____

11. Calve's disease of lumbosacral region   _____

12. Acute hematogenous osteomyelitis, left humerus   _____

13. Osteitis deformans of left fingers _____

14. Osteolysis of right tibia _____

15. Hypertrophy of left ulna _____

16. Adult osteochondrosis of right knee _____

17. Acquired hallux varus of left foot _____

18. Wrist drop of right hand _____

19. Acquired bow leg of left side _____

20. Chondromalacia of right patella _____

21. Idiopathic gout, right hand _____

22. Effusion of left hip _____

23. Stiffness of right ankle _____

24. Instability of left elbow _____

25. Right shoulder osteitis condensans _____

26. Kaschin-Beck disease of left shoulder _____

27. Contracture of right elbow _____

28. Recurrent dislocation of left finger _____

29. Fistula of right hand joint _____

30. Flail joint of left knee _____

Diseases of the Genitourinary System

Diseases of both the male and female genitourinary systems are classified to ICD-10-CM Chapter 14. Instructional notations appear throughout the chapter to direct the coder to "use additional codes," to "code first," or to "code also associated underlying conditions." Many of the codes are expanded at the fourth- and fifth-character levels to include specific codes for acute, chronic, or unspecified states of a disease. Codes for diseases that impact the breast include fifth characters to indicate laterality.

Check Your Knowledge of Anatomy and Disorders

Label the figures correctly by using the following terms. Answers are located in Appendix A.

A. Terms for Figure 12-1

Adrenal suprarenal

Left kidney

Left renal artery

Prostate gland

Renal cortex

Renal medulla

Right kidney

Right and left ureters

Ureteral orifices

Urethra

Urethral meatus

Urinary bladder

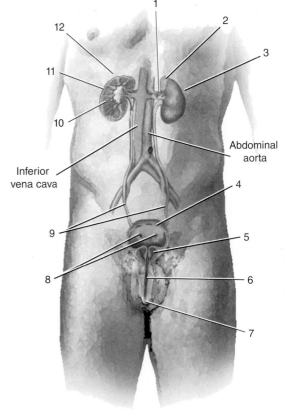

Figure 12-1

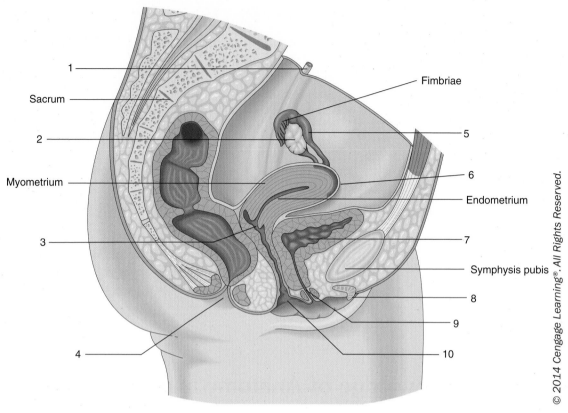

1

Sacrum

2

Myometrium

3

4

Fimbriae

5

6

Endometrium

7

Symphysis pubis

8

9

10

Figure 12-2

B. Terms for Figure 12-2

Anus	Ovary
Body of uterus	Ureter
Cervix of uterus	Urethra
Clitoris	Urinary bladder
Fallopian tube	Vagina

Check Your Clinical Knowledge

Circle one of the selections provided in parentheses to complete the following sentences. Answers are located in Appendix A.

1. An inflammation of the fallopian tube is known as _____. (oophoritis, salpingitis)

2. Patients with end-stage renal disease require _____. (dialysis, insulin)

3. A test used to determine the levels of urea nitrogen or waste products in the blood is a _____ test. (BUN, urine C&S)

4. _____, an inherited disease, causes enlargement of both kidneys due to the formation of multiple grape-like cysts. (Polycystic disease, Renal failure)

5. _____ incontinence occurs when a person is unable to hold urine when he or she coughs, sneezes, or laughs. (Overflow, Stress)

Coding

Assign ICD-10-CM codes to the following. Answers to exercises 1–10 are located in Appendix A, and the remaining answers are provided only to educators through the instructor online companion.

1. Calculus in urethra _____

2. Urinary tract obstruction _____

3. Prostatic stone _____

4. Irregular periods _____

5. Paravaginal cystocele _____

6. Segmental fat necrosis of breast _____

7. Benign cyst of prepuce _____

8. Acquired bladder neck stenosis _____

9. Detrusor muscle hyperactivity _____

10. Acute nephritis _____

11. Interstitial nephritis _____

12. Bilateral small kidney _____

13. Acute salpingitis and oophoritis _____

14. Bilateral vesicoureteral-reflux with reflux nephropathy with hydroureter _____

15. Stage III chronic kidney disease   _____

16. Renal tubular acidosis   _____

17. Trigonitis with hematuria   _____

18. Chronic interstitial cystitis with hematuria   _____

19. Single spermatocele of epididymis   _____

20. Mammary duct ectasia of left breast   _____

21. Right breast fibroadenosis   _____

22. Breast atrophy   _____

23. Chronic salpingitis   _____

24. Bartholin's gland abscess   _____

25. Intestinal endometriosis   _____

26. Hemoglobin nephrosis   _____

27. Obstructive uropathy   _____

28. Chronic interstitial nephritis   _____

29. Cyst of prostate   _____

30. Solitary cyst of left breast   _____

Pregnancy, Childbirth, and the Puerperium

Chapter 15 of ICD-10-CM classifies conditions occurring during pregnancy, childbirth, and the puerperium as well as encounters for the supervision of high-risk pregnancies. Codes from this chapter of ICD-10-CM are used only for coding of the records of mothers. Seventh characters are used for some codes to identify multiple gestations. The trimester in which the condition occurs is identified for some codes.

A code from category Z37, Outcome of Delivery, should be included on every maternal record when a delivery has occurred. These codes are not to be used on subsequent records or on the newborn record.

Check Your ICD-10-CM Knowledge

Circle one of the selections provided in parentheses to complete the following sentences. Answers are located in Appendix A.

1. ICD-10-CM defines the _____ trimester from 14 weeks 0 days to less than 28 weeks 0 days. (second, third)

2. A seventh character of 0 for code O33.5xx0 denotes _____. (single gestation, fetus 1)

3. Obstetric _____ is reported with code O71.7. (hematoma of vulva, damage to coccyx)

4. _____ is classified to code O00.1. (Rupture of fallopian tube due to pregnancy, Mural pregnancy)

5. A young primigravida, as defined by ICD-10-CM, is a woman who is less than _____ years old at expected date of delivery. (16, 18)

Check Your Clinical Knowledge

Circle one of the selections provided in parentheses to complete the following sentences. Answers are located in Appendix A.

1. The most common location of an ectopic pregnancy is the _____. (fallopian tubes, cervix)

2. Excessive vomiting during pregnancy is known as _____. (hyperemesis gravidarum, miscarriage)

3. _____ is the abnormal positioning of the placenta in the lower uterus. (Abruptio placentae, Placenta previa)

4. The letters in HELLP syndrome refer to _____, elevated liver function, and low platelet level. (hypertension, hemolysis)

5. Pre-eclampsia is a serious condition of pregnancy characterized by hypertension, _____, and proteinuria. (coma, edema)

Coding

Assign ICD-10-CM codes to the following. Answers to exercises 1–10 are located in Appendix A, and the remaining answers are provided only to educators through the instructor online companion. For this exercise, assign an Outcome of Delivery code when prompted.

1. Missed abortion at 17 weeks' gestation with retention of dead fetus _____

2. 24-week OB visit for 14-year-old primigravida patient _____

3. Tubal abortion _____

4. Eclampsia during 29th week of pregnancy _____

5. Antepartum hemorrhage with coagulation defect at 30 weeks' gestation _____

6. Diabetes mellitus arising during pregnancy controlled by diet _____

7. Premature separation of placenta with afibrinogenemia, at 31 weeks' gestation _____

8. *Streptococcus* group A infection of bladder following delivery _____

9. Cracked nipple due to breast-feeding _____

10. Cesarean delivery of 7-pound 11-ounce baby girl *(assign an Outcome of Delivery code)* _____

11. 30-week gestational patient with pre existing hypertension complicating the pregnancy _____

12. Triplet pregnancy at 35 weeks' gestation with transverse presentation of fetus three _____

13. Annular detachment of the cervix complicating delivery _____

14. Delayed delivery after artificial rupture of membranes _____

15. Obstetric hematoma of vagina complicating delivery _____

16. Rupture of uterus before onset of labor at 16-week gestation _____

17. Placenta percreta, 18 weeks _____

18. Braxton Hicks contractions _____

19. UTI following induced termination of pregnancy _____

20. Obstetric fat embolism, 35 weeks _____

21. Primary agalactica _____

22. Puerperal thyroiditis _____

23. Gonorrhea complicating pregnancy at 12 weeks _____

24. Anemia complicating pregnancy at 19 weeks _____

25. Physical abuse complicating pregnancy at 8 weeks _____

26. Puerperal galactocele _____

27. Elective agalactia _____

28. Hemorrhoids in the puerperium _____

29. Puerperal phlebopathy _____

30. Postpartum blues _____

Certain Conditions Originating in the Perinatal Period and Congenital Malformations, Deformations, and Chromosomal Abnormalities

Conditions originating in the fetal or perinatal period (before birth through the first 28 days after birth) are classified to Chapter 16 of ICD-10-CM. These codes are used on the records of the newborns. Chapter 17 of ICD-10-CM classifies congenital malformations, deformations, and chromosomal abnormalities. Codes from this chapter are not for use on maternal or fetal records.

Check Your Knowledge of Conditions

From the following conditions listed, place a checkmark in front of the diagnostic statement if it reflects congenital malformations, deformations, or chromosomal abnormalities. Answers are located in Appendix A.

_____ **1.** Pentalogy of Fallot

_____ **2.** Respiratory distress syndrome

_____ **3.** Sepsis of newborn due to *E. coli*

_____ **4.** Cleft palate with bilateral cleft lip

_____ **5.** Neonatal cerebral ischemia

_____ **6.** Transposition of colon

_____ **7.** Complex syndactyly of fingers with synostosis

_____ **8.** Traumatic glaucoma of newborn

_____ **9.** Neonatal melena

_____ **10.** Van der Woude's syndrome

Check Your Clinical Knowledge

Circle one of the selections provided in parentheses to complete the following sentences. Answers are located in Appendix A.

1. _____ is a congenital disorder in which the posterior portion of the vertebrae of the bony spinal column fails to close over the spinal cord. (Cerebral palsy, Spina bifida)

2. _____ is a combination of four defects of the heart. (Tetralogy of Fallot, Hemophilia)

3. _____ typically impacts the sigmoid colon and is due to an absence of nerves therefore causing a lack of peristalsis. (Hypospadias, Hirschsprung's disease)

4. Congenital varicella is a congenital _____ disease. (bacterial, viral)

5. _____ occurs early in gestation and is a severe form of neural tube deficit with the failure of the cephalic aspect of the neural tube to close. (Anencephaly, Talipes equinovarus)

Coding

Assign ICD-10-CM codes to the following. Answers to exercises 1–10 are located in Appendix A, and the remaining answers are provided only to educators through the instructor online companion.

1. Lumbar spina bifida with hydrocephalus   _____

2. Rupture of the liver due to birth injury   _____

3. Newborn impacted by in utero exposure to tobacco smoke   _____

4. Newborn type II, respiratory distress syndrome   _____

5. Cephalhematoma due to birth injury   _____

6. Congenital funnel chest   _____

7. Birth weight of newborn, 525 grams   _____

8. Acidosis of newborn   _____

9. Transient neonatal diabetes mellitus   _____

10. Neonatal rectal hemorrhage   _____

11. Congenital accessory eye muscle   _____

12. Congenital pneumonia due to *Staphylococcus*   _____

13. Ostium primum atrial septal defect, type I   _____

14. Hypospadias with intersex state   _____

15. Translocation, trisomy 18   _____

16. Megalocornea with glaucoma   _____

17. Congenital stenosis of larynx   _____

18. Newborn affected by prolapsed cord   _____

19. Mild HIE   _____

20. Sodium balance disturbance of newborn   _____

21. Meconium ileus   _____

22. Neonatal peritonitis   _____

23. Neonate potassium balance disturbance   _____

24. Esophageal reflux of neonate   _____

25. Noninfective mastitis of newborn   _____

26. Newborn affected by forceps delivery   _____

27. Partial atelectasis of newborn   _____

28. Apnea of prematurity   _____

29. Congenital retinal aneurysm   _____

30. Congenital hepatomegaly   _____

Symptoms, Signs, and Abnormal Clinical and Laboratory Findings, Not Elsewhere Classified

CHAPTER 15

Chapter 18 of ICD-10-CM is used to report the following:

- Cases for which no specific diagnosis can be made even after all the facts bearing on the case have been investigated
- Signs or symptoms existing at the time of initial encounter that proved to be transient and whose causes could not be determined
- Provisional diagnosis in a patient who failed to return for further investigation or care
- Cases referred elsewhere for investigation or treatment before the diagnosis has been made
- Cases in which a more precise diagnosis was not available for any other reason
- Certain symptoms, for which supplementary information is provided, that represent important problems in medical care in their own right

Check Your Knowledge

For the symptoms and signs listed next state the main body system (e.g., digestive system) that would be associated with the condition. Answers are located in Appendix A.

    1. Precordial friction _____

    2. Nocturia _____

    3. Pruritus _____

    4. Dyspnea _____

    5. Dysphagia _____

Check Your Clinical Knowledge

Match the abnormal finding with the disease that the finding could indicate. Answers are located in Appendix A.

  _____ **1.** elevated PSA   **A.** seizure activity

  _____ **2.** abnormal EKG   **B.** visual impairment

  _____ **3.** abnormal EEG   **C.** prostate cancer

_____ **4.** abnormal ERG   **D.** diabetes mellitus

_____ **5.** elevated fasting glucose   **E.** myocardial infarction

Coding

Assign ICD-10-CM codes to the following. Answers to exercises 1–10 are located in Appendix A, and the remaining answers are provided only to educators through the instructor online companion.

1. Elevated CRP   _____

2. Fluid retention   _____

3. Painful urination   _____

4. Spastic gait   _____

5. Abnormal bowel sounds   _____

6. Abnormal level of cocaine in the blood   _____

7. Abnormal liver function study   _____

8. Elevated levels of steroids in urine   _____

9. Decreased sexual desire   _____

10. Patient is a 10-day-old infant with excessive crying   _____

11. Night sweats   _____

12. Postprocedural fever   _____

13. Weak urinary stream   _____

14. Elevated glucose tolerance   _____

15. Idiopathic vasovagal attack   _____

16. Senile debility   _____

17. Painful respiration   _____

18. Inability to swallow   _____

19. Abnormal result of Mantoux test   _____

20. Excessive thirst   _____

21. Abnormal weight loss   _____

22. Elevated erythrocyte sedimentation rate   _____

23. Increased fasting glucose   _____

24. Recurrent convulsions   _____

25. Postimmunization fever   _____

26. Tingling skin   _____

27. Poor urinary stream   _____

28. Penile discharge   _____

29. Prerenal uremia   _____

30. Change in mental status   _____

Injuries, Poisoning, and Certain Other Consequences of External Causes

Chapter 19 of ICD-10-CM is used to report injuries, poisonings, and certain other consequences of external causes. For most of the codes found in this chapter, ICD-10-CM seventh characters are used. The final character typically identifies an initial encounter, subsequent encounter, or sequelae. Prior to code selection, coders need to review not only medical documentation but also any reports of X-rays and imaging to support more specificity in the coding assignment.

Check Your Knowledge of Anatomy

Label Figure 16-1 correctly by using the following terms. Answers are located in Appendix A.

Carpals

Clavicle

Femur

Fibula

Humerus

Ilium

Ischium

Mandible

Maxilla

Metacarpals

Metatarsals

Patella

Phalanges of foot

Phalanges of hand

Pubis

Radius

Ribs

Skull

Sternum

Tarsals

Tibia

Ulna

Vertebral column

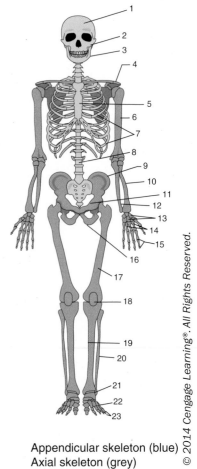

Appendicular skeleton (blue)
Axial skeleton (grey)

Figure 16-1

Coding

Assign ICD-10-CM codes to the following. Answers to exercises 1–10 are located in Appendix A, and the remaining answers are provided only to educators through the instructor online companion. For each exercise, assume an initial encounter unless it is otherwise noted in the diagnostic statement.

1. Complete traumatic amputation of left ear   _____

2. Subsequent encounter for puncture wound of the scalp   _____

3. Right eye, penetrating wound of orbit   _____

4. Posterior displaced Type II dens fracture, subsequent encounter
    with routine healing   _____

5. Contusion of left front wall of thorax   _____

6. Rejection of bone marrow transplant   _____

7. Sexual abuse of child   _____

8. Local infection due to port-a-cath   _____

9. Open transverse fracture of the shaft of the right femur, displaced   _____

10. Sprain in left hip iliofemoral ligament, third follow-up visit   _____

11. Crushing injury of right thigh   _____

12. Laceration of right knee with foreign body   _____

13. Sprain of lateral collateral ligament of left knee   _____

14. Displaced bile duct prosthesis   _____

15. Necrosis of amputated stump of left arm   _____

16. Shock from electric current   _____

17. Dislocation of right clavicle   _____

18. Open wound of right ankle, subsequent encounter   _____

19. Traumatic partial amputation between hip and knee on the
    right side of body   _____

20. Poisoning by ampicillin, accidental   _____

21. Dislocation of mandible   _____

22. Patient seen in ER for abrasion of throat   _____

23. Subsequent visit for concussion of thoracic spinal cord   _____

24. Blister on left shoulder   _____

25. Splinter in left knee   _____

26. Crushing injury of face, subsequent encounter   _____

27. Laceration of diaphragm, initial encounter   _____

28. Traumatic hemothorax, initial encounter   _____

29. Foreign body in colon, subsequent encounter   _____

30. Avulsion of spleen   _____

External Causes of Morbidity

Chapter 20 of ICD-10-CM is used to report environmental events and circumstances that are the cause of injury and other adverse effects. These codes are to be used as secondary codes to describe the circumstance that was the external cause of morbidity. The following table provides an overview of the types of codes that appear in this chapter. Note that codes with four or five characters that require a seventh-character extension will be completed with the use of "x" placeholders.

Codes	Description (assume all encounters are the initial encounter)
V02.01xA	Pedestrian on roller-skates injured in collision with two- or three-wheeled motor vehicle in nontraffic accident
W21.01xA	Struck by football
W93.01xA	Contact with dry ice
X98.2xxA	Assault by hot fluids

Check Your Knowledge

Refer to the beginning of the Tabular section of Chapter 20 and reference the definitions of transport vehicles. For each statement below, complete the missing term that relates to definitions for transport accidents. For example, special construction vehicles include bulldozers, diggers, earth levelers, dump trucks, backhoes, front-end loaders, pavers, and mechanical shovels. Answers are located in Appendix A.

1. A hot-air balloon is a type of _____ device.

2. A bus is a motor vehicle designed to carry more than _____ passengers.

3. A _____ accident is any vehicle accident that occurs entirely in any place other than a public highway.

4. A motor-driven tricycle or a motorized rickshaw is considered a _____ motor vehicle.

5. A person changing a tire that is involved in an accident is considered a _____.

Coding

Assign ICD-10-CM V00-Y99 codes for the following statements. Do not assign the code for the injury. This exercise is to practice the selection of External Causes of Morbidity codes from Chapter 20 of ICD-10-CM. Assign Place of Occurrence (Y92) and Activity codes (Y93) when prompted in the exercise. For assignment of seventh-character extension, assume initial encounter unless otherwise stated. Answers to exercises 1–10 are located in Appendix A, and the remaining answers are provided only to educators through the instructor online companion.

1. Tripping over carpet at patient's single family home in bedroom while rough housing *[in addition to an External Cause code, assign a code for both the Place of Occurrence (Y92-) and Activity (Y93-)]* _____

2. Bitten by horse _____

3. Fall into hole _____

4. Gored by goat _____

5. Hypodermic needle stick _____

6. Subsequent encounter due to helicopter crash causing injury to occupant _____

7. Tree accidentally falling on person _____

8. Injury from walking into lamppost, subsequent encounter _____

9. Struck by softball _____

10. Evaluation of injury to foot by being skated over by sharp skate blades _____

11. Suicide attempt by hanging _____

12. Injuries from an assault caused by being pushed in front of a train _____

13. Injury by cigar burn _____

14. Cut from broken glass _____

15. Driver of car injured as a result of a collision with a van on downtown street _____

16. Skin damage due to exposure to sunlight, subsequent visit _____

17. Skin damage caused by tanning bed _____

18. Suicide attempt by cutting right leg with knife   _____

19. Accidental suffocation in burning building   _____

20. Accidental drowning in swimming pool at the neighborhood community
pool *[in addition to an External Cause code, assign a code for both
the Place of Occurrence (Y92-) and Activity (Y93-)]*   _____

21. Fall out of bed   _____

22. Seven-year-old jumped into water and sustained multiple injuries   _____

23. Injury from nail gun   _____

24. Stepped on by elephant   _____

25. Gunshot wound   _____

26. Assault by handgun discharge, initial encounter   _____

27. Burn by electric blanket, initial encounter   _____

28. Bitten by sheep, initial encounter   _____

29. Building collapse object striking person, initial encounter   _____

30. Effects of hot weather, initial encounter   _____

Factors Influencing Health Status and Contact with Health Services

The reasons for encounters are reported in ICD-10-CM with the use of Z codes that are found in Chapter 21 of ICD-10-CM. These codes are reported to indicate that a person may or may not be sick but encounter health care services for a specific purpose, or to indicate a circumstance or problem that influences the person's health status but is not in itself a current illness or injury. Instructional notations that instruct coders to "Use additional codes" or "Code first" are present throughout the chapter.

Check Your Knowledge

For each statement state whether the statement is true (T) or false (F). Answers are located in Appendix A.

_____ **1.** Category codes from Z37, Outcome of Delivery, would be reported on the newborn's record.

_____ **2.** Codes from Chapter 21 of ICD-10-CM can be reported only as secondary codes.

_____ **3.** When a patient has an encounter for a medical examination and an abnormal finding is documented, the coder should report a code for the medical examination and the finding.

_____ **4.** Separate code categories exist for encounters for medical observations and encounters for screenings.

_____ **5.** Only one code is reported from Chapter 21 of ICD-10-CM when a child is seen for a routine childhood examination and immunization.

Coding

Assign ICD-10-CM Z codes for the cases. Answers to exercises 1–10 are located in Appendix A, and the remaining answers are provided only to educators through the instructor online companion.

1. Carrier of typhoid _____

2. Type AB, Rh-negative blood _____

3. Patient seen in the office for a sports physical _____

4. Screening for HPV _____

5. Occupational exposure to dust _____

6. Problems related to child living in a group home _____

7. Lack of adequate sleep   _____

8. Underachievement in school   _____

9. History of estrogen therapy   _____

10. Encounter for checking of IUD   _____

11. Patient admitted for cosmetic procedure   _____

12. History of malignant neoplasm of the rectum   _____

13. Counseling for sexual education   _____

14. Family history of leukemia   _____

15. Patient had a vasectomy 3 years earlier   _____

16. Patient has a partial artificial right arm (status)   _____

17. Patient seen in the physician's office for removal of postsurgical
    abdominal drain   _____

18. Adjustment of infusion pump   _____

19. Whole blood donor   _____

20. Adjustment of cerebral ventricular shunt   _____

21. Adult health checkup, no findings   _____

22. Hearing examination following failed hearing screening   _____

23. Paternity testing   _____

24. Observation for alleged adult rape, ruled out   _____

25. Carrier of hepatitis B surface antigen [HbsAg]   _____

26. Personal history of thrombophlebitis   _____

27. Encounter for attention to colostomy   _____

28. History of UTI   _____

29. Holiday relief care   _____

30. Bedridden   _____

Transition from ICD-9-CM to ICD-10-CM

Transitioning from ICD-9-CM to ICD-10-CM will have a great impact on the health care industry. To facilitate the transition, the National Centers for Health Statistics has developed Diagnosis Code Set General Equivalence Mappings (GEM) to be used as a translational tool. The GEM presents the information in an easy-to-use table format that maps ICD-9-CM codes to ICD-10-CM codes. It should be noted that there is not always a one-to-one mapping of codes. Coders cannot use the GEM in place of the ICD-10-CM code book. The GEM files can be found on the NCHS website at http://www.cdc.gov/nchs/icd/icd10cm.htm#10update. The files contain the codes without the code titles and were designed to be used by the health care industry for the creation of mapping applications.

Coding

For each statement that follows, assign the correct ICD-9-CM and ICD-10-CM codes. Answers to exercises 1–10 are located in Appendix A, and the remaining answers are provided only to educators through the instructor online companion.

1. Open wound of the nose, initial visit
   ICD-9-CM: _____
   ICD-10-CM: _____

2. Congenital salivary fistula
   ICD-9-CM: _____
   ICD-10-CM: _____

3. Acute tonsillitis
   ICD-9-CM: _____
   ICD-10-CM: _____

4. Collapsed lung
   ICD-9-CM: _____
   ICD-10-CM: _____

5. Lung mass
   ICD-9-CM: _____
   ICD-10-CM: _____

6. Bronchial stenosis
   ICD-9-CM: _____
   ICD-10-CM: _____

7. Chronic hepatitis C
   ICD-9-CM: _____
   ICD-10-CM: _____

8. Alcohol withdrawal
   ICD-9-CM: _____
   ICD-10-CM: _____

9. Panic disorder
   ICD-9-CM: _____
   ICD-10-CM: _____

10. Obsessive-compulsive disorder
    ICD-9-CM: _____
    ICD-10-CM: _____

11. Portal hypertension
    ICD-9-CM: _____
    ICD-10-CM: _____

12. Herniated cervical disc, mid-cervical region
    ICD-9-CM: _____
    ICD-10-CM: _____

13. Initial visit for closed rib fracture on right side
    ICD-9-CM: _____
    ICD-10-CM: _____

14. Ulcerative colitis
    ICD-9-CM: _____
    ICD-10-CM: _____

15. Rheumatoid arthritis
    ICD-9-CM: _____
    ICD-10-CM: _____

16. Second visit for fatigue fracture of right fibula with routine healing
    ICD-9-CM: _____
    ICD-10-CM: _____

17. Infarction of spleen
    ICD-9-CM: _____
    ICD-10-CM: _____

18. Obstruction of gallbladder
    ICD-9-CM: _____
    ICD-10-CM: _____

19. Congenital polycystic kidney
    ICD-9-CM: _____
    ICD-10-CM: _____

20. Calculus of kidney
ICD-9-CM: _____
ICD-10-CM: _____

21. Prostatic hemorrhage
ICD-9-CM: _____
ICD-10-CM: _____

22. Endometriosis of uterus
ICD-9-CM: _____
ICD-10-CM: _____

23. Uterine cyst
ICD-9-CM: _____
ICD-10-CM: _____

24. Endometriosis of ovary
ICD-9-CM: _____
ICD-10-CM: _____

25. Restricting type of anorexia nervosa
ICD-9-CM: _____
ICD-10-CM: _____

26. Hyperemesis gravidarum, at week 19
ICD-9-CM: _____
ICD-10-CM: _____

27. Delivery of single child complicated by prolapse of cord
ICD-9-CM: _____
ICD-10-CM: _____

28. Supervision of normal first pregnancy at 6 weeks
ICD-9-CM: _____
ICD-10-CM: _____

29. Aortic valve stenosis
ICD-9-CM: _____
ICD-10-CM: _____

30. Second visit for whiplash injury
ICD-9-CM: _____
ICD-10-CM: _____

31. Initial visit for traumatic pneumothorax
ICD-9-CM: _____
ICD-10-CM: _____

32. Encounter of palliative care
ICD-9-CM: _____
ICD-10-CM: _____

33. Encounter for hearing examination following failed hearing screening

ICD-9-CM: _____

ICD-10-CM: _____

34. Preoperative cardiovascular examination

ICD-9-CM: _____

ICD-10-CM: _____

35. Threatened premature labor at 30 weeks, not delivered

ICD-9-CM: _____

ICD-10-CM: _____

36. Cellulitis of finger

ICD-9-CM: _____

ICD-10-CM: _____

37. Seborrheic dermatitis

ICD-9-CM: _____

ICD-10-CM: _____

38. Cervical spondylosis with myelopathy

ICD-9-CM: _____

ICD-10-CM: _____

39. Cervical postlaminectomy syndrome

ICD-9-CM: _____

ICD-10-CM: _____

40. Rotator cuff syndrome of right shoulder

ICD-9-CM: _____

ICD-10-CM: _____

41. Postlaminectomy kyphosis

ICD-9-CM: _____

ICD-10-CM: _____

42. Spina bifida with hydrocephalus

ICD-9-CM: _____

ICD-10-CM: _____

43. Newborn affected by knot in cord

ICD-9-CM: _____

ICD-10-CM: _____

44. Chronic respiratory distress occurring in the perinatal period

ICD-9-CM: _____

ICD-10-CM: _____

45. Hemolytic disease of newborn

ICD-9-CM: _____

ICD-10-CM: _____

46. Neonatal dehydration
  ICD-9-CM: _____
  ICD-10-CM: _____

47. Anemia of prematurity
  ICD-9-CM: _____
  ICD-10-CM: _____

48. Enlargement of lymph nodes
  ICD-9-CM: _____
  ICD-10-CM: _____

49. Sequelae of complete lesion L4 of lumbar spinal cord
  ICD-9-CM: _____
  ICD-10-CM: _____

50. Late effect of physeal fracture or upper end of right femur
  ICD-9-CM: _____
  ICD-10-CM: _____

Coding with ICD-10-PCS

ICD-10-PCS is unique in its format and organization. The system was developed to replace Volume III (procedure codes) in ICD-9-CM. ICD-10-PCS codes were designed to identify hospital inpatient procedures; however, providers may elect to use the codes for other data collection purposes. The Centers for Medicare & Medicaid Services (CMS) requires ICD-10-PCS codes only for inpatient services. The classification system includes seven characters, each character representing an aspect of the procedure. For example, the first character represents the section, which may indicate Medical/Surgical, Obstetrics, or Mental Health.

The workbook exercises are designed in a step-by-step approach for building a code by focusing on the selection of individual characters that comprise the entire code. The last exercise will allow practice for assigning the entire ICD-10-PCS code. The following is a snapshot of an ICD-10-PCS code, illustrating the building blocks for the seven characters.

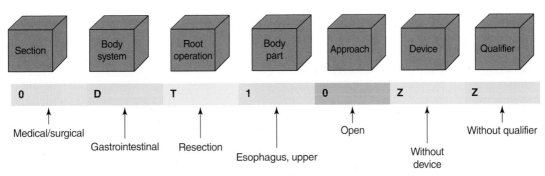

Figure 20-1

United States Department of Health & Human Services. (2011). Retrieved from http://www.cms.gov/ICD10/Downloads/pcs_whats_new_2011.pdf

Format and Organization of ICD-10-PCS

The format of ICD-10-PCS is designed around *Root Operations*. Root operations describe the *intent or reason* for the surgical procedure. For example, complete removal of the thyroid gland is classified to the root operation Resection, but taking a piece of tissue (biopsy) of the thyroid gland is classified to the root operation Excision. There are thirty-one (31) root operations that describe surgical procedures. Coders need to be able to differentiate between each root operation and apply the full definition.

Coding Illustration

The coding process begins with analyzing the documentation and applying definitions and official coding guidelines. Note the step-by-step approach listed next:

1. Analyze documentation

2. Select root operation

3. Reference alphabetic index

4. Build code from PCS Table

The following is an illustration of the PCS coding process that begins with analyzing the documentation in an excerpt of an Operative Report.

OPERATIVE REPORT

PREOPERATIVE DIAGNOSIS: Appendicitis

POSTOPERATIVE DIAGNOSIS: Gangrenous appendicitis

PROCEDURE PERFORMED: Laparoscopic converted to open appendectomy

FINDINGS: Patient had gangrenous appendicitis with perforation

DESCRIPTION OF PROCEDURE: The patient was prepped and draped in the usual fashion. A 5-mm 30-degree laparoscope was inserted. A Foley catheter was placed preoperatively. A 5-mm trocar was placed in the suprapubic region and one placed in the left lower quadrant. The patient was noted to have gangrenous appendicitis, and I was unable to mobilize the appendix laparoscopically. The decision was made to covert to an open procedure. The trocars were then removed under visualization of the laparoscope.

A standard Rockey-Davis incision was made in the right lower quadrant. We entered the peritoneal cavity just lateral to the rectus abdominus muscle. The base of the appendix was tied off with 2-0 Vicryl tie. The mesoappendix was taken down and was tied off with 2-0 Vicryl ties. The appendix was amputated and sent to Pathology.

Hemostasis was achieved with electrocautery and the transversalis was closed with 2-0 Vicryl in a running fashion. The external oblique was closed with a 0 Vicryl in a running fashion. The wound was irrigated and closed with staples. The infraumbilical fascia was approximated with a 0 Vicryl in interrupted fashion. The skin was closed with staples.

1. *Analyze the documentation.* What procedures were performed?

   Answer: Laparoscopic appendectomy converted to open.

   What guideline governs the decision to code both the open approach and laparoscopic approach?

   Answer: Guideline B3.2 (section d) for Multiple Procedure—"During the same operative episode, multiple procedures are coded if the intended root operation is attempted using one approach, but is converted to a different approach." Therefore, the decision is to code the procedure twice, using different approach values from character 5 in the PCS code.

2. *Select Root Operation.* Based on the coder's knowledge of definitions, the root operation RESECTION is chosen because the whole body part was taken.

3. *Reference Alphabetic Index.* Under the root operation Resection, search for Appendix for the first four characters of the code assignment: 0DTJ.

4. *Build Code from PCS Table.* Refer to the table 0DTJ (Medical Surgical, Gastrointestinal System, Resection, Appendix). Build the code based on the approach, device, and qualifier (if applicable).

5. *Answer based on the documentation.*

   0DTJ0ZZ (Resection of Appendix, Open Approach)

   0DTJ4ZZ (Resection of Appendix, Percutaneous Endoscopic Approach)

Further study and knowledge of the PCS coding system and surgical procedures will assist with the coding process. For example, insertion of the Foley catheter, use of electrocautery to prevent bleeding, and the suturing to close the wound are all an integral part of the operation and not assigned a separate PCS code.

Alphabetic Index

ICD-10-PCS (referred to as PCS) provides an Alphabetic Index to guide coders to the appropriate section of the code book Tables. In addition, the Index provides classification reference for body parts and devices. The Index is a **tool** but coders must rely on their knowledge of format and organization and master the definitions of Root Operations before attempting to code. The Alphabetic Index may provide the entire seven-digit character for the complete code or a portion of the code to reference in the Tables. Coders must always check the PCS Tables for the final decision. A review of the Alphabetic Index will reveal that the organization is based on Root Operations (e.g., Excision, Resection) as well as instructional notes for other terms.

Examples of Instructional Notes:

Body Part Guidance:

Prodisc-C   *use* Synthetic Substitute

Medial popliteal nerve   *use* Nerve, Tibial

Root Operation Guidance:

Graft

    see Replacement

    see Supplement

        (This entry asks the coder to review the documentation to determine if the graft was used as a Replacement or Supplement. These Root Operations will be discussed in a later exercise.)

The instructional notes support consistent application of definitions and help to support the integrity of the classification system.

Alphabetic Index Exercise

Search the Alphabetic Index for the following procedures, body parts, or devices. Document the instructional note. Answers to exercises 1–5 are located in Appendix A, and the remaining answers are provided only to educators through the instructor online companion.

1. Incision, abscess   _____

2. PTCA   _____

3. Lumpectomy   _____

4. Hepatogastric ligament   _____

5. Chorda tympani   _____

6. Clipping, aneurysm   _____

7. Quadrate lobe   _____

8. Posterior scrotal nerve   _____

9. Colonic Z-Stent   _____

10. Radial collateral ligament   _____

Reading the ICD-10-PCS Tables

The Alphabetic Index is designed to lead the coder to the PCS Table to make the final coding selection. The following case study will help to explain the workflow for selecting the correct PCS code based on definitions and use of both the Alphabetic Index and PCS Table.

Case Study:

The surgeon documents that a percutaneous needle drainage was performed to remove excessive fluid from the liver. The drainage tube was necessary for continuous drainage and will remain in the patient at the conclusion of the procedure. As a first step, search the Alphabetic Index for *Drainage, Liver* which provides the first four characters of the code (0F90). Reference PCS Table (Figure 20-2) to see that the decision making begins with the Approach column. The definitions for the Root Operations, Approaches, Devices, and Qualifiers will be the focus of future workbook activities, but this lesson will serve as an overview. The documentation that the procedure was performed with a needle indicates a percutaneous approach; therefore, the fifth character will be 3-Percutaneous. Next, review the coding selections for the last two columns: Device and Qualifier. Note that the exact same body parts and approaches are repeated in different rows.

Official ICD-10-PCS Coding Guidelines (see Appendix E) **A9** states that within a PCS table, valid codes include all combinations of choices in characters 4 through 7 contained in the same row of the table.

In other words, coders should not choose characters from different rows of the PCS Table. The format of the rows guides the coder to make appropriate choices. In this case, the choices are guiding the coding selection based on if the intent for the drainage procedure was for diagnostic or therapeutic reasons. The surgeon inserted the tube for continuous drainage, for excessive fluid; therefore, this indicates it was performed for therapeutic purposes and the Device would be 0.

Note that the last column for Qualifier does not provide an option for "X" (Diagnostic). It would be an invalid code if the character 0 (Drainage Device) would be selected with a Qualifier of "X"—for diagnostic. The diagnostic procedure would require a sample of fluid for laboratory analysis and this was not the intent of this procedure.

The correct coding assignment for this case study would come from the top row of the table: 0F9030Z

Section	0	Medical and surgical
Body system	F	Hepatobiliary system and pancreas
Operation	9	Drainage: Taking or letting out fluids and/or gases from a body part

Body part	Approach	Device	Qualifier
0 Liver **1** Liver, right lobe **2** Liver, left lobe **4** Gallbladder **G** Pancreas	**0** Open **3** Percutaneous **4** Percutaneous endoscopic	**0** Drainage device	**Z** No qualifier
0 Liver **1** Liver, right lobe **2** Liver, left lobe **4** Gallbladder **G** Pancreas	**0** Open **3** Percutaneous **4** Percutaneous endoscopic	**Z** No device	**X** Diagnostic **Z** No qualifier

Figure 20-2

United States Department of Health & Human Services. (2011). Retrieved from http://www.cms.gov/ICD10/Downloads/pcs_whats_new_2011.pdf

PCS Table Exercise

Refer to Figure 20-3 to answer the following questions. Assign PCS codes using the table. All answers are located in Appendix A.

1. The surgeon performed a craniotomy to insert a neurostimulator generator within the skull bone of the patient _____

2. Insertion of percutaneous growth stimulator in the skull _____

Section	0	Medical and surgical
Body system	N	Head and facial bones
Operation	H	Insertion: Putting in a nonbiological appliance that monitors, assists, performs, or prevents a physiological function but does not physically take the place of a body part

Body part	Approach	Device	Qualifier
0 Skull	**0** Open	**4** Internal fixation device **5** External fixation device **M** Bone growth stimulator **N** Neurostimulator generator	**Z** No qualifier
0 Skull	**3** Percutaneous **4** Percutaneous endoscopic	**4** Internal fixation device **5** External fixation device **M** Bone growth stimulator	**Z** No qualifier

Figure 20-3

United States Department of Health & Human Services. (2011). Retrieved from http://www.cms.gov/ICD10/Downloads/pcs_whats_new_2011.pdf

Character 1: Section

For inpatient surgical procedures, the majority of the codes will be selected from the Medical and Surgical section that begins with the numeric character 0. The Medical and Surgical Related Sections begin with the Obstetrics section (1) and continue with a variety of sections, including Measurement and Monitoring (4), Imaging (B), and Mental Health (H).

The following list displays all of the sections in ICD-10-PCS. This exercise will explore the organization of this first character for coding.

Sections

0- Medical and Surgical	8- Other Procedures
1- Obstetrics	9- Chiropractic
2- Placement	B- Imaging
3- Administration	C- Nuclear Medicine
4- Measurement and Monitoring	D- Radiation Oncology
5- Extracorporeal Assistance and Performance	F- Physical Rehabilitation and Diagnostic Audiology
6- Extracorporeal Therapies	G- Mental Health
7- Osteopathic	H- Substance Abuse Treatment

Section Exercise

Using the Alphabetic Index and the excerpt for Sections listed in the previous table, write the character that represents the section in ICD-10-PCS on the line that is provided. Answers to exercises 1–5 are located in Appendix A, and the remaining answers are provided only to educators through the instructor online companion.

1. _____ Hypothermia treatment (whole body)
2. _____ Fetal pulse oximetry
3. _____ Nasal packing
4. _____ Narcosynthesis
5. _____ Spiritual group counseling for treatment of cocaine abuse
6. _____ Beam radiation of the pancreas
7. _____ CT scan of the cervical spine (low osmolar)
8. _____ Blood transfusion–red blood cells (infused via central artery)
9. _____ Hysteroscopy
10. _____ Monitoring of urinary flow

Character 2: Body System

Character 2 in ICD-10-PCS is reserved for "Body System." The following is a subset for body systems in the Medical and Surgical section.

Body Systems

5- Upper Veins

6- Lower Veins

7- Lymphatic and Hemic Systems

8- Eye

9- Ear, Nose, Sinus

C- Mouth and Throat

D- Gastrointestinal System

F- Hepatobiliary System and Pancreas

J- Subcutaneous Tissue and Fascia

P- Upper Bones

Q- Lower Bones

W-Anatomical Regions

Body System Exercise

The second character in ICD-10-PCS represents the body systems, which also includes anatomical regions. Using the subset listed in the preceding box, write the correct character that classifies the body system for the following procedures on the line provided. Use the Alphabetic Index as your guide for this exercise. Answers to exercises 1–5 are located in Appendix A, and the remaining answers are provided only to educators through the instructor online companion.

Example: Mediastinoscopy (Alphabetic Index provides the second character "W" which represents Anatomical Regions.)

1. _____ Right hemicolectomy
2. _____ Scapulectomy
3. _____ Dilation of left lacrimal duct
4. _____ Percutaneous mechanical thrombectomy—femoral vein
5. _____ Laparoscopic cholecystectomy
6. _____ Inspection of peritoneal cavity
7. _____ Esophagoscopy for removal of foreign body
8. _____ Total sinus ethmoidectomy
9. _____ Splenectomy
10. _____ Insertion of pacemaker generator in subcutaneous tissue of chest

Character 3: Root Operation

The Root Operation represents the third character position in the ICD-10-PCS code. Identification of the Root Operation is a key decision-making component for the code selection. Coders must determine the intent of the procedure for an accurate selection of the root operation. Appendix C includes a list of Root Operations and definitions, explanations, and examples to guide coder decisions. There are a total of 31 Root Operations that are divided into 9 general categories. The following outline displays the nine categories and their corresponding Root Operations:

1. Take Out Some or All of a Body Part
   - *Excision, Resection, Extraction, Destruction, Detachment*

2. Put In/Put Back or Move Some or All of a Body Part

   • *Transplantation, Reattachment, Reposition, Transfer*

3. Take Out or Eliminate Solid Matter, Fluids, or Gases from a Body Part

   • *Drainage, Extirpation, Fragmentation*

4. Involve Only Examination of Body Parts and Regions

   • *Inspection, Map*

5. Alter the Diameter/Route of a Tubular Body Part

   • *Bypass, Dilation, Occlusion, Restriction*

6. Always Involve a Device

   • *Insertion, Replacement, Supplement, Removal, Change, Revision*

7. Involve Cutting or Separation Only

   • *Division, Release*

8. Define Other Repairs

   • *Control, Repair*

9. Define Objectives

   • *Alteration, Creation, Fusion*

In the decision-making process, first consider the nine categories instead of the entire suite of 31 Root Operations. For example, if the main intent of the procedure is to insert a feeding tube, the choices of Root Operations would fall under category 6: Always Involve a Device. The following decision tree (Figure 20-4) exhibits the process for distinguishing between the three Root Operations that are in the category for procedures that Take Out or Eliminate Solid Matter, Fluids, or Gases from a Body Part: Drainage, Extirpation, and Fragmentation.

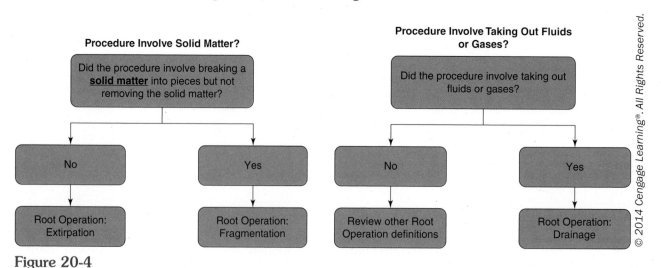

Figure 20-4

Root Operation Exercise 1

For this exercise, distinguish between the three Root Operations from the category That Take Out or Eliminate Solid Matter, Fluids or Gases from a Body Part. Use Appendix C to compare the definitions for Drainage, Extirpation, and Fragmentation. In addition, refer to the decision trees in Figure 20-4. All of the answers are located in Appendix A.

1. Lithotripsy for calculus of the right ureter   _____

2. Esophagoscopy for removal of a chicken bone from the throat   _____

3. Thoracentesis for drainage of fluid from pleural cavity   _____

4. ESWL for kidney stone   _____

5. Thrombectomy   _____

Excision vs. Resection

ICD-10-PCS Coding Guideline A11 states the following:

"Many of the terms used to construct PCS codes are defined within the system. It is the coder's responsibility to determine what the documentation in the medical record equates to in the PCS definitions. The physician is not expected to use the terms used in PCS code descriptions, nor is the coder required to query the physician when correlation between documentation and the defined PDS terms is clear.

Example: When the physician documents 'partial resection' the coder can independently correlate 'partial resection' to the root operation Excision without querying the physician for clarification."

Source: Centers for Medicare and Medicaid Services, www.cms.hhs.gov

This coding guideline is emphasized in differentiating between the root operations Excision and Resection. Physicians use many terms to describe taking out tissue, such as biopsy, removal, and excision. It is the coder's responsibility to translate the documentation to support the selection of the root operation.

For this second exercise on Root Operations, the focus will be on distinguishing between the two of the five Root Operations from the category That Take Out Some or All of a Body Part: Excision and Resection. Use Appendix C to compare the definitions between Excision and Resection. Excision is defined as cutting out or off, without replacement, a *portion* of a body part. An example would be removing a colon polyp or performing a wedge resection of the lung. Resection is cutting out or off, without replacement, *all* of a body part. Although this appears to be straightforward, this process is more difficult because coders must reference the Alphabetic Index for guidance and PCS Tables for final determination. The PCS Body Part Key is integrated in the PCS Alphabetic Index and it helps to distinguish if a body part can be assigned with the root operation of Resection.

Note the following coding guideline:

Guideline B3.8 Excision vs. Resection

PCS contains specific body parts for anatomical subdivisions of a body part, such as lobes of the lungs or liver and regions of the intestine. Resection of the specific body part is coded whenever all of the body part is cut out or off, rather than coding Excision of a less specific body part.

The following decision process will help to differentiate between Excision and Resection. Note that the step includes referring to the Alphabetic Index to determine if there is a selection for Resection of a body part.

Did the surgeon cut out or off, without replacement, a portion of a body part?

Although this is the definition for Excision, the next step is to analyze if a subdivision of a body part can be "resected" in PCS. As mentioned in Guideline B3.8, subdivisions of body parts may be resected. During early training, coders will not be familiar with the classification of excision vs. resection; therefore, it is necessary to review the Alphabetic Index for guidance. For example, if the surgeon states that the right upper lobe of the lung was removed, the coder must check in the Alphabetic Index to determine if there is a unique body part entry for resection of the right upper lobe in the Index. Note the following Alphabetic Index entry:

> Resection
>
> Lung
>
> Upper Lobe
>
> Right 0BTC

Because PCS provides an entry for coding resection of this portion of the lung, Resection is the correct Root Operation.

Excision vs. Resection Example:

The procedure the surgeon performed was "removal of the antrum of the stomach." Note that in the Alphabetic Index, there is no entry under Resection of the antrum of the stomach; therefore, the correct Root Operation is Excision. The surgeon removed a subdivision of a body part (stomach), but this subdivision is not classified as such under Resection in the Alphabetic Index. In addition, the PCS Table would not provide a selection under Resection. Note the following Alphabetic entry for the first four characters of the code:

> Excision
> Stomach 0DB6

Root Operation Exercise 2

Refer to the root operation Resection in Alphabetic Index to determine if the following procedures on subdivisions of body parts are classified as Excision or Resection. If the procedure is not located in the index under Resection, refer to Excision. Write the correct PCS partial characters (three or four characters) and indicate if it was found under the Root Operation *Excision* or *Resection*. Answers to exercises 1–3 are located in Appendix A, and the remaining answers are provided only to educators through the instructor online companion.

1. Excision of the pylorus of the stomach   _____

2. Removal of the lingula of the bronchus   _____

3. Removal of the tail of the pancreas   _____

4. Resection of the left lobe of the liver   _____

5. Excision of left adrenal gland _____

6. Removal of the lower esophagus _____

7. Excision of the distal section of the jejunum _____

Root Operation Exercise 3

Reference Appendix C to assign Root Operations for the following procedures. Only assign Root Operations; do not attempt to assign codes at this point. Answers to exercises 1–5 are located in Appendix A, and the remaining answers are provided only to educators through the instructor online companion.

1. Adjustment of displaced pacemaker lead _____

2. Corneal transplant _____

3. ERCP with balloon dilation of common bile duct _____

4. Closed reduction of distal radical fracture _____

5. Fetal spinal tap, open _____

6. Laparoscopic vaginal hysterectomy _____

7. Lumpectomy, left breast _____

8. Diagnostic colonoscopy _____

9. Placement of central venous catheter _____

10. Liposuction of thighs (cosmetic) _____

11. Postpartum bilateral tubal ligation _____

12. Removal of a leiomyosarcoma of the stomach _____

13. Extracorporeal shock wave lithotripsy of ureter _____

14. Laparoscopy with lysis of adhesions _____

15. Percutaneous endoscopic gastrostomy (PEG) tube change _____

16. Diagnostic left thoracentesis _____

17. Laparoscopic inguinal herniorrhaphy _____

18. Right groin sentinel lymph node biopsy _____

19. Interbody spinal fusion at L3-4 and L4-5 _____

20. Removal of retained intrauterine contraceptive device _____

21. Repair of ventral hernia with use of mesh _____

22. Removal of a piece of hard candy lodged in the throat _____

23. Total hip arthroplasty _____

24. Roux-En-Y gastric bypass _____

25. Nissen's fundoplication for gastroesophageal reflux disease _____

26. Episiotomy _____

27. Placement of ventricular shunt for patient with hydrocephalus _____

28. Suturing of lacerated tendon _____

29. Debridement of necrotic skin ulcer _____

30. Amputation of little finger _____

Character 4: Body Part

The fourth character in ICD-10-PCS identifies the specific body part for the procedure. There are two main resources for guidance with selecting the correct body part:

1. Reference the Alphabetic Index under the name of body part for classification.

2. Reference the PCS Table for final coding decision.

The next two exercises will focus on the use of these two resources.

Body Part Exercise 1

For the Body Part Exercise 1, refer to the Alphabetic Index for the appropriate body part classification. Write the body part reference term. Follow the body part reference term to locate the first several characters under the documented Root Operation.

For example: The surgeon documents that he performed a division of the left hamate bone. Searching under the Root Operation-Division, note that there is no entry for hamate bone. Reference the term Hamate bone in the Alphabetic Index and note that it states to classify to Carpal, left. Next, in the Alphabetic Index, reference Division, Carpal, Left for the first four characters: 0P8N.

All of the answers are located in Appendix A.

1. _____ Transfer of the left extensor hallucis brevis muscle

2. _____ Excision of medial plantar nerve

3. _____ Repair of the right circumflex iliac artery

Body Part Exercise 2

For the Body Part Exercise 2, refer to the following excerpt from the ICD-10-PCS Table for the Root Operation *Excision* in the body system *Gastrointestinal* (Figure 20-5). For visualization of the

Section	0	Medical and surgical
Body system	D	Gastrointestinal system
Operation	B	Excision: Cutting out or off, without replacement, a portion of a body part

Body part	Approach	Device	Qualifier
1 Esophagus, upper 2 Esophagus, middle 3 Esophagus, lower 4 Esophagogastric junction 5 Esophagus 6 Stomach, pylorus 7 Small intestine 8 Duodenum A Jejunum B Ileum C Ileocecal valve E Large intestine F Large intestine, right	0 Open 3 Percutaneous 4 Percutaneous endoscopic 7 Via Natural or artificial opening 8 Via Natural or artificial opening endoscopic	Z No device	X Diagnostic Z No qualifier

Figure 20-5

*United States Department of Health & Human Services. (2011). Retrieved from
http://www.cms.gov/ICD10/Downloads/pcs_whats_new_2011.pdf*

anatomic body parts, refer to Appendix B of this workbook. Rely on your knowledge of anatomy to assist with this exercise. Write the character for the body part (e.g., character 5 for Esophagus) on the line that is provided. All of the answers are located in Appendix A.

1. _____ The surgeon excised a polyp from the first portion of the small intestine.

2. _____ A biopsy was performed from the region of the stomach where it connects to the esophagus.

3. _____ The surgeon excised a lesion located on the sphincter muscle that connects the small intestine to the large intestine.

Character 5: Approach

The Approach character identifies the surgical technique used to reach the procedure site. This information will come from the documentation in the Operative Report. CMS provides definitions for the approaches (as well as other unique characters) on its Web site. The following table identifies the most common approaches with definitions for the medical/surgical cases.

Medical and Surgical Approach Definitions

Approach	Definition
External	Procedures performed directly on the skin or mucous membrane and procedures performed indirectly by the application of external force through the skin or mucous membrane.
Open	Cutting through the skin or mucous membrane and any other body layers necessary to expose the site of the procedure.
Percutaneous	Entry, by puncture or minor incision, of instrumentation through the skin or mucous membrane and any other body layers necessary to reach the site of the procedure.
Percutaneous endoscopic	Entry, by puncture or minor incision, of instrumentation through the skin or mucous membrane and any other body layers necessary to reach and *visualize* the site of the procedure.
Via natural or artificial opening	Entry of instrumentation through a natural or artificial external opening to reach the site of the procedure.
Via natural or artificial opening endoscopic	Entry of instrumentation through a natural or artificial external opening to reach and *visualize* the site of the procedure.
Via natural or artificial opening with percutaneous endoscopic assistance	Entry of instrumentation through a natural or artificial external opening and entry, by puncture or minor incision, of instrumentation through the skin or mucous membrane and any other body layers necessary to aid in the performance of the procedure.

Approach Exercise 1

View the following surgical illustrations (Figures 20-6 through 20-10) and match the visual with the definitions of approaches listed in the previous table. All of the answers are located in Appendix A.

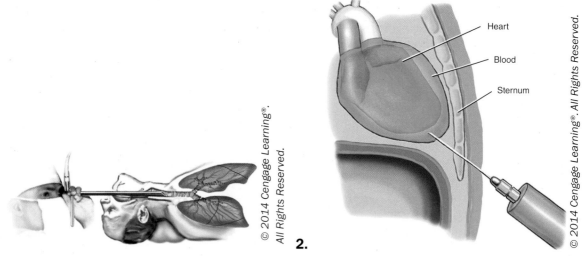

1.

Figure 20-6 Rigid bronchoscopy

2.

Figure 20-7 Cardiac tamponade: pericardial aspiration with needle and syringe

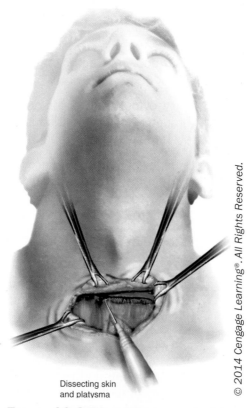

3.

Dissecting skin and platysma

Figure 20-8 Thyroidectomy: Incision

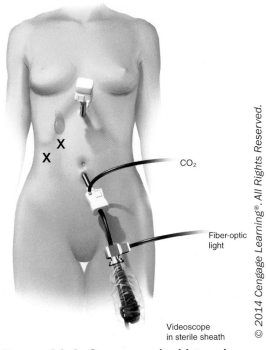

4.

Figure 20-9 Camera and additional trocars are placed

Videoscope in sterile sheath

CO₂

Fiber-optic light

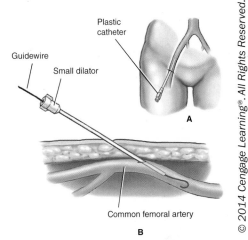

Plastic catheter

Guidewire

Small dilator

A

Common femoral artery

B

5.

Figure 20-10 Intra-aortic balloon pump insertion: (A) Needle cannula assembly is inserted into femoral artery, (B) small dilator is threaded over guidewire

Approach Exercise 2

Apply the Medical and Surgical Approach Definitions to the following procedures. Identify if the procedure is percutaneous, percutaneous endoscopic, via natural or artificial opening, via natural or artificial opening endoscopic, or via natural or artificial opening with percutaneous endoscopic assistance. Answers to exercises 1–5 are located in Appendix A, and the remaining answers are provided only to educators through the instructor online companion.

1. Esophagogastroduodenoscopy (EGD) _____
2. Open reduction of distal tibia fracture _____
3. Sterile dressing applied to the wound of the shoulder _____
4. Thyroidectomy _____
5. Colonoscopy _____
6. Laparoscopic appendectomy _____
7. Digital rectal examination _____
8. Total abdominal hysterectomy _____
9. Endotracheal intubation _____
10. Percutaneous bone marrow biopsy _____

Approach Exercise 3

This exercise includes excerpts from Operative Reports that describe the approach. Review the documentation and refer to the definitions to classify the approach. If you are unfamiliar with the procedure, perform a Web search that further describes the technique. Write the name of the approach next to the excerpt. Answers to exercises 1–3 are located in Appendix A, and the remaining answers are provided only to educators through the instructor online companion.

1. Description of procedure: The patient was brought emergently to the cardiac catheterization lab. Sedation was given with a total of 250 mcg of fentanyl and 5 mg of versed. Local anesthesia was given in the right groin with 1% lidocaine. The right common femoral artery was accessed using the modified Seldinger technique, and a 6-French sheath was placed.

_____

2. The patient had general anesthesia and positioned supine; the right knee was prepped and draped in the routine fashion. The knee was elevated and tourniquet inflated to 300 mmHg. A midline incision was opened over the patella and sharp dissection carried down to the extensor mechanism.

_____

3. The patient was taken to the operating room and was induced with general endotracheal anesthesia. The abdomen was prepped and draped in sterile fashion. An umbilical incision was made and a Veress needle was introduced and abdomen was insufflated to 3 liters. A **10** mm supraumbilical trocar was introduced with a Visiport. Under direct visualization, two right lateral and one left-sided trocar were introduced.

_____

4. The colonoscope was inserted via the anus and advanced under direct vision until the cecum was reached.

_____

5. After careful consideration of the area, appropriate needle placement was found and marked. The area was then sterilely prepped and draped in the usual fashion with chlorhexidine swab. The area was then anesthetized with 10cc of 1% lidocaine. A #11 blade was used to make a small skin nick, through which an 8-French, 18-gauge needle/ catheter system was advanced under direct guidance into the fluid collection system.

_____

6. The patient was prepped and draped in sterile fashion and 20 mL of 0.25% Marcaine with epinephrine was used to inject the skin. A 10-blade scalpel was used to skin incision and the prior craniotomy flap was reflected anteriorly and held in place with fishhooks over a Ray-Tec sponge. The temporalis muscle was also reflected anteriorly so that the perimeter of the craniotomy flap could be identified.

_____

7. After this patient was prepped and draped, I began by placing a 21-French rigid cystoscope with a 12-degree lens into the urethra and bladder.

_____

8. A standard sternotomy incision was made and the pericardium was opened longitudinally and T'd at the diaphragm.

_____

9. The base of the tongue was palpated and no indurated masses could be felt. He was examined with a laryngoscope. His larynx was noted to be normal.

_____

10. The patient had a skin ulcer that required superficial debridement.

_____

Character 6: Device

The sixth character appears only in sections that are applicable; otherwise, the default of Z (no device) is assigned. Definitions are provided by CMS and classification guidance is provided from the Alphabetic Index. Only devices that remain in place at the conclusion of the procedure are coded. Exploration of PCS Tables will reveal consistent terminology (classification) such as intraluminal, extraluminal, and internal fixation.

Device Exercise 1

To maintain consistency in the classification system, the Alphabetic Index provides numerous references for common surgical devices. Refer to the Alphabetic Index to determine the classification for the following devices. Answers to exercises 1–4 are located in Appendix A, and the remaining answers are provided only to educators through the instructor online companion.

Example:

If the surgeon documents that a Mark IV Breathing Pacemaker System was inserted in the subcutaneous tissue and fascia of the chest, what device value would be selected from the 0JH table (see excerpt in Figure 20-11)?

```
0 Monitoring device, hemodynamic
2 Monitoring device
4 Pacemaker, single chamber
5 Pacemaker, single chamber rate
   responsive
6 Pacemaker, dual chamber
7 Cardiac resynchronization pacemaker
   pulse generator
8 Defibrillator generator
9 Cardiac resynchronization defibrillator
   pulse generator
A Contractility modulation device
B Stimulator generator, single array
C Stimulator generator, single array
   rechargeable
D Stimulator generator, multiple array
E Stimulator generator, multiple array
   rechargeable
H Contraceptive device
M Stimulator generator
N Tissue expander
P Cardiac rhythm related device
V Infusion device, pump
W Vascular access device, reservoir
X Vascular access device
```

Figure 20-11

United States Department of Health and Human Services. (2012). Retrieved from http://www.cms.gov/ICD10

Answer: Refer to Mark IV Breathing Pacemaker System in the Alphabetic Index, which states to "use Stimulator Generator in Subcutaneous Tissue and Fascia." Based on this reference, the correct PCS value from the device column would be "M."

1. Formula™ Balloon-Expandable Renal Stent System   _____

2. Ex-PRESS™ mini glaucoma shunt   _____

3. Stratos LV Pacemaker Generator   _____

4. Nitinol framed polymer mesh   _____

5. Cobalt/chromium head and socket   _____

6. Bard® Dulex™ mesh   _____

7. Paclitaxel-eluting peripheral stent   _____

8. InterStim® Therapy lead   _____

Device Exercise 2

Refer to the following excerpt from a table in ICD-10-PCS (Figure 20-12) and identify the device (tissue substitutes) described in the following procedures. Research any unfamiliar terms using the Web. All of the answers are located in Appendix A.

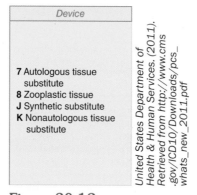

Figure 20-12

1. Repair of bladder with tissue that was created from the patient's own intestinal tissue

_____

2. A laboratory-produced skin tissue was used on the burn victim

_____

3. Mitral valve replacement with porcine tissue

_____

Character 7: Qualifier

The last character in ICD-10-PCS is called a qualifier. The qualifiers provide additional information and are used only in certain sections; the default is Z for "no qualifier." In a previous exercise, the Qualifier "X" was used to identify a Diagnostic procedure. For the following exercise, refer to the ICD-10-PCS Table 0SR excerpt for hip joint replacement (Figure 20-13).

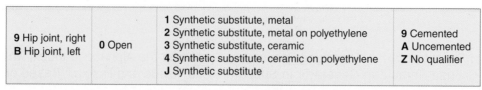

| 9 Hip joint, right
B Hip joint, left | 0 Open | 1 Synthetic substitute, metal
2 Synthetic substitute, metal on polyethylene
3 Synthetic substitute, ceramic
4 Synthetic substitute, ceramic on polyethylene
J Synthetic substitute | 9 Cemented
A Uncemented
Z No qualifier |

Figure 20-13

Qualifier Case Study

This case is a Replacement of the left hip joint. Refer to the Root Operation Replacement and search for Joint, Hip, Left. The Alphabetic Index provides the first four characters (OSRB). It is an open procedure; therefore, decisions need to be made only for the Device and Qualifier. From the following documentation, complete the codes with choosing the correct Device and Qualifier. Answer is located in Appendix A.

OPERATIVE NOTE

PREOPERATIVE DIAGNOSIS: Left severe hip arthritis.

POSTOPERATIVE DIAGNOSIS: Left severe hip arthritis.

PROCEDURE: Press-fit total hip arthroplasty.

Femoral head and neck were removed and sent to pathology for review. The ball and socket of the hip joint were replaced with titanium prosthesis and polyethylene surface. What is the appropriate code for this case?

Building an ICD-10-PCS Code

Assign ICD-10-PCS codes to the following procedures. Answers to exercises 1–5 are located in Appendix A, and the remaining answers are provided only to educators through the instructor online companion.

1. Bilateral liposuction of upper arms (elective procedure) _____

2. Laparoscopic-assisted total vaginal hysterectomy (LAVH) _____

3. Advancement flap skin graft covering left forearm _____

4. Open reduction with internal fixation, displaced left lateral ankle fracture _____

5. ERCP with balloon dilation of common bile duct _____

6. Needle biopsy of liver, right lobe _____

7. Debridement-excision of right hip pressure ulcer down to and including the subcutaneous layer and fascia _____

8. Colonoscopy with removal of polyp using hot biopsy forceps in ascending colon. The surgeon explained that the polyp looked suspicious and was awaiting pathological analysis. _____

9. Complete thyroidectomy, open _____

10. Repair of left thumb, flexor pollicis longus tendon _____

Coding Operative Reports

Assign ICD-10-PCS codes to the procedures documented in the following Operative Reports. Answers to exercises 1–5 are located in Appendix A, and the remaining answers are provided only to educators through the instructor online companion.

OPERATIVE REPORT 1

PREOPERATIVE DIAGNOSIS: Abnormal right mammogram.

POSTOPERATIVE DIAGNOSIS: Abnormal right mammogram.

PROCEDURE PERFORMED: Right breast lumpectomy.

ESTIMATED BLOOD LOSS: Minimal.

INDICATIONS FOR PROCEDURE: The patient had an area of abnormal thickening noted on a mammogram, just lateral to the nipple–areolar complex.

DESCRIPTION OF THE PROCEDURE: The patient was taken to the operating room and placed in the supine position. After general endotracheal anesthesia was administered, the patient was prepped and draped in the usual sterile manner.

The patient had a right lateral circumareolar incision made. A generous lumpectomy was performed around this area. There were no dominant masses. The specimen was removed and sent to pathology. The biopsy cavity was inspected, and hemostasis was achieved. The dermal tissue was reapproximated with 3-0 Polysorb in an interrupted fashion. The skin was closed with a 4-0 Caprosyn in a running subcuticular fashion. The wound was infiltrated with 0.5% Marcaine and 1% lidocaine. The patient had Steri-Strips and a sterile dressing applied.

The patient was awakened from anesthesia, having suffered no apparent intraoperative complications.

ICD-10-PCS Code(s): _____

OPERATIVE REPORT 2

PREOPERATIVE DIAGNOSIS: Unstable left distal radial metaphyseal fracture.

POSTOPERATIVE DIAGNOSIS: Unstable left distal radial metaphyseal fracture.

PROCEDURE PERFORMED: Open reduction and internal fixation of left distal radius.

ANESTHESIA: General.

PROCEDURE IN DETAIL: After obtaining informed consent, the patient was brought to the operating room whereupon the smooth induction of general anesthesia was performed. The patient was positioned in a supine fashion on the operating room table and all bony prominences were well padded. The left upper extremity was placed on a radiolucent arm board. A tourniquet was placed in the left upper extremity, and the left upper extremity was prepped and draped in a standard sterile fashion from the distal arm to the fingertips. After exsanguination of the left upper extremity with an Ace wrap, the tourniquet was inflated to 200 mmHg.

A 6-cm incision was made over the volar aspect of the wrist just radial to the flexor carpi radialis (FCR) tendon, which was palpable. The skin was dissected sharply and the subcutaneous tissue was dissected bluntly down to the level of the antebrachial fascia. This was incised sharply in line with the incision under direct visualization. The FCR tendon and median nerve were retracted in an ulnar direction. The radial artery and attendant leash of veins were retracted in a radial direction. In this manner the pronator quadratus was identified. It was released from its radial insertion to expose the volar aspect of the distal radius. The distal radial transverse metaphyseal fracture was thus visualized. This fracture was mobilized with a Freer and reduction was checked with intraoperative fluoroscopy in the AP and lateral views. After mobilization of this callus, a three-hole Synthes-locked distal radial plate was selected and contoured to fit the volar aspect of the distal radius. Holding the plate slightly off the radial shaft, three locking screws were placed through the plate and into the distal fragment just below the subchondral bone. Once these screws were in place, the plate was brought down onto the radial shaft, thus achieving the reduction. The plate was held in position with 3.5-mm fully threaded standard cortical screws. Reduction was checked on AP and lateral views and found to be anatomic.

The wound was then copiously irrigated with normal saline and closed. The skin was then closed using interrupted 4-0 nylon suture in a horizontal mattress fashion. A sterile dressing and a well-padded, well-molded sugar-tong splint were placed.

The patient was awoken from anesthesia and taken to the recovery room in stable condition.

ICD-10-PCS Code(s): _____

OPERATIVE REPORT 3

PROCEDURE PERFORMED: Esophagogastroduodenoscopy with cautery.

INDICATIONS: Gastrointestinal (GI) bleed and angiodysplasia of the stomach.

PREOPERATIVE DIAGNOSES: GI bleed and angiodysplasia of the stomach.

POSTOPERATIVE DIAGNOSES: GI bleed and angiodysplasia of the stomach.

INSTRUMENT AND MEDICATIONS: The Olympus video system was used. The patient was given a total of 2 mg of IV Versed and 25 mcg of IV fentanyl. Throat was sprayed and epinephrine as well as bipolar cautery was used.

DESCRIPTION OF THE PROCEDURE: The scope was passed through the hypopharynx with ease. The esophagus, stomach, and duodenum to the second portion were all well evaluated, including retroflexion of the GE junction from below. The findings were within normal limits in the duodenum and the esophagus, but in the stomach I could see one spot of angiodysplasia. This was injected with approximately 1.5 mL of 1:10,000 epinephrine. It blanched rather nicely. I then used the Gold probe and on a setting of 16 watts using 2-second pulses. I was able to fulgurate this. The patient tolerated the procedure well.

ICD-10-PCS Code(s): _____

OPERATIVE REPORT 4

PREOPERATIVE DIAGNOSIS: Screening for colon cancer.

POSTOPERATIVE DIAGNOSIS: Normal colon to the level of the cecum.

PROCEDURE: Colonoscopy.

ANESTHESIA: Titrated increments of fentanyl and Versed.

COMPLICATIONS: None.

DESCRIPTION OF PROCEDURE: The patient was brought to the endoscopy suite where he was confirmed to be in stable condition. His history and physical examinations were essentially unchanged from the time of dictation. His questions were again addressed prior to initiation of the procedure. With confirming of hemodynamic stability, the patient was given titrated increments of fentanyl and Versed to achieve IV sedation.

The colonoscope was introduced and I was able to navigate through to the level of the cecum, with clear visualization of the ileocecal valve. The scope was then very carefully brought back for careful inspection and readvancement of the scope to ensure good visualization. With careful inspection and withdrawal time of approximately 10 minutes, the scope was then retroflexed and then withdrawn.

Overall, the patient tolerated the procedure well and he is stable to recovery.

FINDINGS: Normal colon to the level of the cecum.

ICD-10-PCS Code(s): _____

OPERATIVE REPORT 5

PREOPERATIVE DIAGNOSIS: Right nasal foreign body.

POSTOPERATIVE DIAGNOSIS: Right nasal foreign body.

DESCRIPTION OF THE PROCEDURE: This patient was placed in the supine position under satisfactory general anesthesia by mask. His nose was examined and a small cotton foreign body was removed from the anterior aspect of the nose. This seemed to be the entire content of the foreign body and his nose was examined and no further foreign body was noted. He was then awakened and taken to recovery in satisfactory condition.

ICD-10-PCS Code(s): _____

OPERATIVE REPORT 6

PROCEDURE: Thoracentesis.

INDICATION: Large fluid collection on the left side.

CONSENT: Informed consent was obtained from the patient. The risks, benefits, and alternatives to the procedure were explained, and the patient agreed to proceed with thoracentesis.

DESCRIPTION OF THE PROCEDURE: The left posterior lower thorax was cleansed with iodine. Using standard sterile technique, the fluid was identified with a fine needle in a place of dullness. Subsequently, the skin was incised with a scalpel for about 2 mm. Catheter was inserted over the needle in the pleural cavity without difficulty. Opaque greenish-colored fluid was collected in suction bottles; 1.9 liters of fluid was removed, and at the end of the procedure, intermittent drainage occurred, and eventually the drainage stopped, at which time the tube was removed and the procedure was terminated. The patient had some cough while the fluid was being removed. Overall, he tolerated the procedure very well, and there were no complications.

ICD-10-PCS Code(s): _____

OPERATIVE REPORT 7

DIAGNOSIS: Pneumonia with severe hypoxemia.

PROCEDURE: Endotracheal intubation.

Patient was sedated with Versed 3 mg, Fentanyl 25 mcg, and Etomidate 10 mg. Patient was intubated with 8.0 ETT using the Glidescope with direct visualization of vocal cords. Patient tolerated the procedure well without complications.

ICD-10-PCS Code(s): _____

OPERATIVE REPORT 8

PREOPERATIVE DIAGNOSIS: Incisional hernia.

POSTOPERATIVE DIAGNOSIS: Incisional hernia.

PROCEDURE: Laparoscopic incisional herniorrhaphy with mesh.

INDICATIONS: The patient is a 70-year-old gentleman who has previously undergone a vertical-banded gastroplasty and this was converted to a Roux-en-Y gastric bypass. He has had a single midline incision and now has developed a painful mass in his epigastrium. Clinical evaluation and CT scanning has confirmed the diagnosis of a symptomatic incisional hernia and he will now undergo repair.

FINDINGS: Incisional hernia, not incarcerated.

PROCEDURE IN DETAIL: The patient was brought to the operating room and placed supine on the operating table. General endotracheal anesthesia was induced and his abdomen was prepped and draped sterilely. Then 0.25% Marcaine was infiltrated into his surgical sites for postoperative analgesia.

A small nick was made in the left upper quadrant. A Veress needle was inserted into the abdomen through this nick. After confirming intraabdominal position of the needle, pneumoperitoneum to 15 mmHg was generated. A 5-mm port was placed in the left side of the abdomen using an Optiview technique. Under direct vision, a second right-sided port and a left-sided port were placed. Utilizing these three 5-mm ports, adhesions to the anterior abdominal wall were taken down with combination of sharp dissection and electrocautery. This exposed a Swiss cheese–type hernia defect in the upper portion of his abdomen. All fat and these hernia defects were reduced. Adhesions were taken down up underneath the diaphragm to allow for placement of the mesh into this position. Once this was completed, an 8 inch × 10 inch piece of Physio-mesh was brought to the operating field. A suture was placed in the superior and inferior aspects of the mesh. The superior suture was placed approximately 1 inch from the mesh edge to allow it to be placed in the subxiphoid position and have the mesh flip up underneath the diaphragm to be tacked under the diaphragm. The mesh was then inserted into the abdomen and unfolded. The epigastric suture was brought through counter incisions on the anterior abdominal wall. The intraabdominal pressure was then turned down to 8. The mesh was then stretched inferiorly and a mark was made on the anterior abdominal wall inferiorly where all defects would be covered and the mesh would be tensioned appropriately. A counter incision was made in this location and the preplaced 0 PDS suture was brought through the anterior abdominal wall. These two sutures were held on tension. With the intraabdominal pressure still at 8, two rows of tacks were placed circumferentially through the anterior abdominal wall. To facilitate this, two further 5-mm ports were needed to be placed in the lateral aspects of the abdomen. Once the tacking of the mesh was completed, two more transfascial sutures were placed in the lateral aspects of the mesh. This was done by passing a 0 PDS suture transfascially lateral to the mesh through one of the 5-mm port site incisions. The endo close was then passed through the mesh and the suture grasped and brought back out through the anterior abdominal wall. This was done on both the right and left sides of the abdomen. With the four transfascial sutures now in place, the mesh was inspected and found to be appropriately positioned. All of these sutures were tied. The ports were removed and the pneumoperitoneum released. To facilitate placement of the mesh, one of the 5-mm ports was changed out for an 11-mm port and this port site fascial defect was encircled with an 0 Vicryl suture to occlude its fascial defect. The pneumoperitoneum was released by removing the remainder of the ports. The skin incisions were closed with 4-0 Monocryl subcuticular suture and Steri-Strips. The patient tolerated the procedure well, there were no complications, and estimated blood loss was minimal. He was taken to recovery in satisfactory condition.

ICD-10-PCS Code(s): _____

OPERATIVE REPORT 9

DIAGNOSIS: Super-morbid obesity with a BMI of 59

PROCEDURE: Laparoscopic sleeve gastrectomy

DESCRIPTION OF PROCEDURE: The patient was taken to the operating room and induced with general endotracheal anesthesia. He was placed on a split-leg table. Boney prominences were protected. The abdomen was prepped and draped in sterile fashion. A supraumbilical incision was made, and a Veress needle was introduced. The abdomen was insufflated to 3 liters. A 20 mm Visiport was introduced. A left paramedian 10 mm trocar, and a mirroring right 10 mm were also placed. Two lateral 5 mm trocars and a subxiphoid 5 mm trocar were placed. The liver was retracted with a snake retractor. The left crus of the diaphragm was cleared. Five cm from the pylorus, a suture was placed. Short gastrics were then taken in a sequential fashion using the Harmonic scalpel. The short gastrics up at the EG junction were, really, quite short. With the stomach fully mobilized, Endo GIA was used to create a gastric sleeve along with 34 bougie. The first two firings of the stapler were gold loads followed by green loads with Peri-Strips on all staplers. We were next to the bougie, but blood vessels on each side were preserved. At the EG junction, the staple line was carried a little more laterally to assure ourselves that we were well clear and free from the esophagus. Staple lines were inspected. Hemostasis was assured. The stomach was removed via the left-sided trocar. The abdomen was thoroughly irrigated with saline and hemostasis was reassured. 0 Vicryl was used for fascial closure on the dilated 10 mm trocar, 4-0 PDS used for subcuticular closure all around, with Dermabond applied. The patient was taken to the recovery room in good condition.

ICD-10-PCS Code(s): _____

OPERATIVE REPORT 10

PREOPERATIVE DIAGNOSIS: Retained hardware right tibia with hardware bursitis.

POSTOPERATIVE DIAGNOSIS: Retained hardware right tibia with hardware bursitis.

PROCEDURE: Right tibia hardware removal.

INDICATIONS: This 60-year-old lady underwent intramedullary nailing of her right tibia about a year ago. The patient has since then healed her tibia fracture and had had symptoms reminiscent of hardware bursitis. She is agreeable to the decision to remove the hardware.

PROCEDURE: Under general anesthesia and tourniquet control, the right leg was prepped and draped using normal sterile technique. Prior to surgery the patient's previous incisions were marked for reference. The three short incisions were utilized to remove the transfixing screws. All three screws were easily removed without difficulty. The wounds were irrigated and closed with staples. Next, the patient's longitudinal incision over the medial patellar tendon area was utilized to approach the proximal end of the tibial rod. Soft tissue was cleaned out of the proximal rod and the end cap was easily removed. Once the end cap was removed, the inserter/extractor attachment was inserted into the proximal end of the rod and using a slap hammer the rod was gently removed. The knee wound was irrigated and closed with absorbable sutures repairing the medial retinaculum to the patellar tendon followed by absorbable sutures on the subcutaneous tissues and staples on the skin. A light dressing was applied, one at the knee and the other at the ankle. Tourniquet time was 40 minutes. Blood loss was minimal. There were no complications.

ICD-10-PCS Code(s): _____

OPERATIVE REPORT 11

PREOPERATIVE DIAGNOSIS: Right thyroid mass

POSTOPERATIVE DIAGNOSIS: Right thyroid mass

PROCEDURE: Excision of Thyroid Mass

PROCEDURE IN DETAIL: The patient was taken to the operating room and general anesthesia with orotracheal intubation was performed. The neck was prepped and draped in the usual fashion and a small thyroidectomy incision was sharply incised and superior and inferior subplatysmal flaps were elevated. Dissection down to the thyroid isthmus was performed and then lateral dissection was performed. The mass was noted. It actually looks like the mass was coming off of a pyramidal lobe of the thyroid that was branching off of the superior pole. Capsular dissection around the mass was performed and there was only a small area of attachment to the superior pole of the gland. The mass was removed and submitted for frozen section, which showed a follicular lesion with no obvious malignancy. The remaining gland was palpated and no further masses were noted. Hemostasis was obtained and the wound was closed in three layers. Steri-Strip were used for the skin. No drain was placed. The patient was awakened, extubated, and transported to the recovery room in stable condition.

ICD-10-PCS Code(s): _____

OPERATIVE REPORT 12

DIAGNOSIS: Protrusion of urethral sling tape in vagina

PROCEDURE: Removal of tape

PROCEDURE IN DETAIL: The patient was brought to the operative suite, placed in supine position, given adequate general anesthesia at which time she was converted to the dorsal lithotomy position and prepped about the vulva, vagina, and the perineum with Betadine. She was sterilely draped for the procedure. Examination under anesthesia was carried out. The weighted speculum was placed in the vaginal vault. It was noted that the anterior vaginal mucosa in the distal portion of the vagina was altered in that the most menial 1.5 cm was very thinned out and had a deeper pink coloration. Bordering this laterally, bilaterally, was a thicker slightly more pale pink vaginal mucosa with an edge that appeared to be the original edge that had failed to approximate across the midline. Medial to each of the thicker edges, one could feel the prickly edge of TVT tape sticking out into the vagina ever so slightly. The medial border of the thickened epithelium was grasped with Allis clamps and retracted laterally on the right side first. Metzenbaum scissors were then used to dissect around the edges of the TVT tape that was protruding in this area. The TVT tape was dissected on both its lateral and medial aspects to a depth of approximately 6 or 7 mm. Once this section of TVT tape had been freed up, this small section of TVT tape was removed by cutting it with the Metzenbaum scissors.

An identical procedure was carried out on the patient's left side. Once this was done, the medial aspect of the vaginal mucosa which was very thin was denuded. The lateral vaginal mucosa which was the thicker area was undermined on both sides to a depth of approximately 2.5 cm. The edges of the thickened lateral vaginal mucosa were then drawn together across the midline and reapproximated with a running interlock suture of 3-0 undyed Polysorb. Hemostasis was adequate. Estrace vaginal cream was inserted into the vagina and applied to the wound. The patient was taken to the recovery room in satisfactory condition.

ESTIMATED BLOOD LOSS: 5 cc.

SPECIMENS: Two small pieces of TVT tape each measuring approximately 6–7 mm long.

ICD-10-PCS Code(s): _____

OPERATIVE REPORT 13

PROCEDURE: Diagnostic bronchoscopy

INDICATION: Hemoptysis

PREMEDICATION: The patient received a total of Versed 4 mg, and 50 mcg Fentanyl for conscious sedation.

DESCRIPTION OF PROCEDURE: After applying local anesthetic to the nares and oropharyngeal area, fiberoptic bronchoscopy was passed through the right naris, down to the epiglottis, and the vocal cords, through the vocal cord to the airway. The vocal cord appeared normal. Second, the trachea and carina appear normal, except there are chronic bronchitis changes. Left bronchial tree and right bronchial tree show no interbronchial lesion. There are bronchial mucosa changes consistent with chronic bronchitis. There was no bleeding noticed in the airways and there is no interbronchial lesion.

The patient tolerated the procedure well.

COMPLICATIONS: None.

ICD-10-PCS Code(s): _____

Application of Coding Guidelines

This section is designed to test your knowledge of the ICD-10-CM Official Guidelines for Coding Reporting developed by the Centers for Medicare & Medicaid Services and the National Center for Health Statistics. Answers to exercises 1–10 are located in Appendix A, and the remaining answers are provided only to educators through the instructor online companion.

Instructions: For each question select the appropriate answer.

1. The 32-year-old patient is at a dinner party, drinking wine with her dinner. At 6 PM she takes prescribed Allegra and then experiences severe dizziness and nausea. She is taken to the emergency department to be seen because the symptoms are so severe. After examination the provider concludes that the dizziness and nausea were caused by the combination of the Allegra and wine. This would be reported as a(n):

    a. poisoning.
    b. overdose.
    c. abuse of drugs.
    d. adverse effect.

2. A patient experiencing tachycardia after taking a correct dosage of prescribed Lortab would be reported as a(n):

    a. poisoning.
    b. adverse reaction to a drug.
    c. abuse of drugs.
    d. underdosing.

3. A patient is undergoing hemodialysis for end-stage renal disease in the outpatient department of an acute care hospital. The patient develops what is believed to be severe heartburn, but is sent to observation for several hours, at which time the patient is admitted to inpatient care for further workup. At the time of admission to observation, the admitting physician feels that the patient has unstable angina. The consulting cardiologist diagnoses the patient's problem as a myocardial infarction and the attending physician concurs. What is the principal diagnosis for the acute hospital stay?

    a. Complications of hemodialysis
    b. Myocardial infarction
    c. Unstable angina
    d. Renal disease

4. A patient is admitted for treatment of cough, fever, and congestion. The physician makes the diagnosis of pneumonia. The coder would:

    a. assign codes for cough, fever, congestion, and pneumonia.
    b. assign codes for congestion and pneumonia.
    c. query the physician for the causal relationship between symptoms and pneumonia.
    d. assign code only for pneumonia.

5. A female patient has just undergone a hysterectomy. Documentation indicates that she lost 800 mL of blood during surgery. Her hemoglobin and hematocrit are monitored following surgery. Subsequently she is given a blood transfusion. The physician documents anemia as a secondary diagnosis. The coder would:

    a. query the physician to clarify the type of anemia as acute blood loss.
    b. assign a code for unspecified anemia.
    c. assign a code for acute blood loss anemia.
    d. assign a code for low hemoglobin and hematocrit.

6. The 34-year-old patient is admitted for a compound fracture of the left tibia. He also has superficial abrasions and lacerations in the same area. The coder should:

    a. query the physician to determine if the abrasions and lacerations should be coded.
    b. code the fracture of the tibia only.
    c. code the fracture of the tibia and code the abrasions and lacerations, if treated.
    d. code the fracture, abrasion, and lacerations.

7. Which of the following is **not** considered a poisoning?

    a. Overdose of Oxycontin intentionally taken to commit suicide.
    b. Error made in the administration of the prescribed drug gabapentin by a nurse.
    c. Allergic reaction to Rozerem that was correctly prescribed and properly administered.
    d. Error made in a drug prescription by a physician for Zocar.

8. According to the Official Coding Guidelines, which of the following statements is true in relation to the assignment of code O80?

    a. Code O80 can be assigned with any other codes from Chapter 15 of ICD-10-CM.
    b. Code O80 is always assigned as the principal diagnosis.
    c. When the outcome of delivery is liveborn, twins code O80 can be assigned.
    d. Code O80 can be assigned if the patient had an unresolved antepartum complication at the time of delivery.

9. A fracture of the radius without any further clarification is coded as:

    a. closed and displaced.
    b. closed and nondisplaced.
    c. open and displaced.
    d. open and nondisplaced.

10. An HIV-infected asymptomatic patient is admitted to the hospital as an inpatient with acute appendicitis. A laparoscopic appendectomy is performed. What is the appropriate principal diagnoses code for this case?

    a. AIDS
    b. Acute appendicitis
    c. Admission for surgical procedure
    d. Any of the above

11. The patient is admitted due to anemia associated with colorectal cancer. The patient was transfused and there was no treatment directed at the cancer during this admission. What is the principal diagnosis?

    a. Anemia
    b. Admission for transfusion
    c. Colorectal cancer
    d. Hemorrhagic disorder

12. A patient is admitted with fever, abdominal pain, and an elevated WBC. Acute appendicitis is confirmed. What diagnoses should be reported for this case?

    a. Fever and abdominal pain
    b. Only acute appendicitis
    c. Fever, abdominal pain, and elevated WBC
    d. Acute appendicitis is reported as the principal and fever, abdominal pain, and elevated WBC are reported as secondary diagnoses

13. The following appeared in the documentation for an outpatient visit: Patient's blood pressure is 140/98 mm Hg. The patient has experienced vomiting for three days. The patient was treated for gastritis and the blood pressure will be monitored on the next visit. Which of the following would be correct?
    a. Assign a code for gastritis and hypertension.
    b. Assign a code for gastritis.
    c. Assign a code for gastritis and for high or elevated blood pressure without a firm diagnosis of hypertension.
    d. Assign a code for gastritis, vomiting, and hypertension.

14. The patient has a third-degree burn of the forearm and a second-degree burn on the leg. What is the correct coding action?
    a. Code both burns and sequence the burn of the forearm first.
    b. Code only the burn of the forearm.
    c. Query the physician.
    d. Code both and sequence the leg first.

15. The 28-year-old female was seen in the outpatient department with chronic abdominal pain for the last 7 days. After the examination the physician records: rule out ovarian cyst. What should be coded as the patient's diagnosis?
    a. Observation and evaluation without need for further medical care
    b. Diagnosis of unknown etiology
    c. Ovarian cyst
    d. Abdominal pain

16. When the phrase "code first underlying disease" appears in the ICD-10-CM code book, the coder should:
    a. code the underlying disease only when selecting codes in the inpatient setting.
    b. view this as mandatory depending on the chapter of ICD-10-CM in which the phrase appears.
    c. view this as a mandatory instruction.
    d. treat the phrase as a suggestion only.

17. Given the diagnosis "carcinoma of brain and lymph nodes, metastatic from lungs," what is/are the primary cancer site(s)?
    a. Lungs
    b. Lymph nodes
    c. Lungs and lymph nodes
    d. Brain

18. The 54-year-old female was admitted to the ambulatory care unit for a planned cholecystectomy for cholelithiasis. Shortly before surgery, she developed tachycardia and the surgery was cancelled. After a workup for the tachycardia, she was discharged. The first-listed diagnosis would be a code for:
    a. an encounter for cholecystectomy.
    b. tachycardia.
    c. observation status.
    d. cholelithiasis.

19. The 28-year-old female has had abdominal pain for several weeks and has been spitting up blood for 5 days. She was admitted and the following procedures were completed: abdominal X-ray, CT of abdomen with contrast, and esophagogastroduodenscopy (EGD) with biopsy. The diagnostic testing confirmed gastritis. Which is the principal diagnosis and procedure for this admission?
    a. Abdominal pain, abdominal X-ray
    b. Gastritis, CT of abdomen with contrast
    c. Abdominal pain, EGD with biopsy
    d. Gastritis, EGD with biopsy

20. The patient is seen in the Outpatient Rehabilitation Department for physical therapy after sustaining a fracture of the tibia. The first listed diagnosis for this encounter would come from which of the following coding categories?

    a. Original injury
    b. Encounter for other aftercare
    c. Orthopedic aftercare
    d. Encounter for other postprocedural aftercare

21. An 86-year-old man was admitted for a repair of a hiatal hernia. The hernia was repaired and on the second day of admission the patient fell and fractured his mandible. He also experienced chest pain and dizziness. A cardiac catheterization and percutaneous transluminal coronary angioplasty (PTCA) was completed to rule out cardiac findings. The principal diagnosis is:

    a. chest pain.
    b. dizziness.
    c. hiatal hernia.
    d. fractured mandible.

22. A patient presents with a myocardial infarction with several chronic conditions, including left-side hemiparesis with no further documentation. For coding purposes, the hemiparesis would be classified as:

    a. dominant side
    b. nondominate side
    c. either dominant or nondominate
    d. not otherwise specified

23. A 29-year-old female patient was admitted in active labor. She delivered her fifth child and following the delivery a sterilization procedure was performed for contraceptive reasons. The code for sterilization, Z30.2, would be:

    a. not assigned because it is the same admission as the delivery.
    b. not assigned because it was performed for contraceptive reasons.
    c. assigned as a secondary diagnosis.
    d. assigned as a principal diagnosis.

24. Which of the following is *false* in regards to chronic kidney disease?

    a. Mild chronic kidney disease is reported with code N18.3.
    b. ICD-10-CM classifies chronic kidney disease based on severity.
    c. If both a stage of chronic kidney disease and end-stage renal disease are documented, assign code N18.6 only.
    d. Patients who have undergone kidney transplant may still have some form of CKD; therefore, assign the appropriate N18 code for the patient's stage of CKD and code Z94.0, kidney transplant status.

25. When a patient is admitted for management of dehydration due to a malignancy and only the dehydration is being treated, the coder should:

    a. list the code for the malignancy only.
    b. list the code for dehydration only.
    c. list the code for the malignancy first and then the code for the dehydration.
    d. list the code for the dehydration first followed by the code for the malignancy.

Coding Case Studies

This section of the workbook will allow you to put it all together by selecting codes and following the ICD-10-CM Official Guidelines for Coding and Reporting. Read each case study and for each case select the correct ICD-10-CM and/or ICD-10-PCS codes(s) based on correct coding principles and sequence codes according to the Official Guidelines for Coding and Reporting. Answers to exercises 1–10 are located in Appendix A, and the remaining answers are provided only to educators through the instructor online companion.

1. A 35-year-old female patient was admitted due to heavy uterine bleeding and generalized abdominal pain. A diagnostic hysteroscopy with D&C was completed, which showed bright red blood in the vagina. The discharge diagnosis was uterine cyst and acute blood loss anemia. Select the appropriate codes for this admission.

   ICD-10-CM code(s): _____

   ICD-10-PCS codes(s): _____

2. The patient is 6 weeks post mastectomy for carcinoma of the right breast and is now admitted for chemotherapy. She has no other medical conditions.

   ICD-10-CM code(s): _____

3. The following appeared in the documentation for an outpatient visit:

   Patient's blood pressure is 140/98 mm Hg. There is no documentation of a previous elevated BP. Cardiac: No findings.

   Lungs: No rales, within normal limits.

   Gastrointestinal System: The patient has experienced vomiting for 3 days.

   Assessment: Acute gastritis, elevated BP

   Plan: E prescription sent to pharmacy.

   ICD-10-CM code(s): _____

4. The patient presented for a laparoscopic cholecystectomy due to gallstones. The laparoscopic procedure was started but was converted to an open procedure. Discharge summary was documented:

   Diagnosis: Gallstones

   Procedure: Cholecystectomy

   ICD-10-CM code(s): _____

   ICD-10-PCS code(s): _____

5. This 35-year-old female patient was seen in Dr. Jones' office with a chief complaint of chronic abdominal pain for the last 5 days. After the examination the physician records rule out ovarian cyst and order an ultrasound to be completed at the hospital.
   ICD-10-CM code(s): _____

6. The patient is admitted to an acute care hospital with alcohol withdrawal and is suffering with delirium. The patient has been previously diagnosed with chronic alcoholism. She is being treated for the withdrawal and delirium.
   ICD-10-CM code(s): _____

7. A 55-year-old male was admitted and described as having prolonged and intractable wheezing; airway obstruction that was not relieved by bronchodilators, and lab values showed decreased respiratory function. The discharge summary recorded a final diagnosis of asthma with chronic obstructive pulmonary disease with an acute exacerbation.
   ICD-10-CM code(s): _____

8. The patient was undergoing hemodialysis for end-stage renal disease in the outpatient department of an acute care hospital. After the treatment she complained of severe heartburn and was sent to observation for several hours, at which time the patient is admitted to inpatient care for further workup. The cardiologist diagnoses the patient's problem as unstable angina. The code for the principal diagnosis for the inpatient admission should be:
   ICD-10-CM code(s): _____

9. The patient is admitted with a comminuted displaced fracture of the shaft of the left tibia with multiple abrasions in the same area on his leg. An open reduction of a fracture of the left tibia was performed.
   ICD-10-CM code(s): _____

   ICD-10-PCS code(s): _____

10. A woman, who is a known alcoholic, gave birth via a vaginal delivery to a 5-pound, 3-ounce female infant. The infant was born in the hospital and was diagnosed with fetal alcohol syndrome and remained in the hospital for 3 weeks. At the time of discharge for the infant the codes to report should be:
    ICD-10-CM code(s): _____

11. A 60-year-old patient was admitted with a diagnosis of hyperthyroidism due to ectopic thyroid tissue with thyroid storm. During this admission the patient had an open complete thyroidectomy.
    ICD-10-CM code(s): _____

    ICD-10-PCS code(s): _____

12. An 81-year-old patient is admitted with fever, cough, and shortness of breath. Because of previous concerns a bronchoscopy of the right lung was completed and confirmed pneumonia. Lab testing additionally confirmed a streptococcal, group B, infection. The discharge summary recorded: group B streptococcal pneumonia.
    ICD-10-CM code(s): _____

    ICD-10-PCS code(s): _____

13. A patient was treated for painful urination. A urine test showed a UTI due to *E. coli.*
    ICD-10-CM code(s): _____

14. A 2-year-old child presents to the office today. His mother states that she feels that he has placed an object in his ear. Both ears were examined and there appears to be a foreign object in his right ear. Because of his age he was referred to ENT for further exam and treatment.
ICD-10-CM code(s): _____

15. The patient had a 4-day hospital stay and the discharge diagnoses recorded as:
Principal dx: ASHD, native artery with unstable angina
Secondary dx: type 1 diabetic with diabetic nephropathy
ICD-10-CM code(s): _____

16. The patient presents today with red eyes for the last 2 to 3 days. The patient states that his eyes are becoming more and more irritated. After examination the patient was found to have a chalazion of the right upper eyelid and an infected meibomian gland of the left lower eyelid. Prescriptions were written.
ICD-10-CM code(s): _____

17. A 17-year-old male presents to the emergency department. He was at a party drinking alcohol and accidentally overdosed on speed and vodka tonics. His blood tests showed an alcohol level of 50 mg/100 mL. He was stabilized and referred to the Addiction Unit for evaluation.
ICD-10-CM code(s): _____

18. An 89-year-old patient has resided at Sunny Valley Skilled Nursing Facility for 8 months. The facility physician examined her at the request of the nursing staff. Examination of the skin reveals that there is a chronic ulceration of the skin of the left heel and mid foot. There is no breakdown into the fatty layer, muscle, or bone. This will be monitored by the staff.
ICD-10-CM code(s): _____

19. The patient was seen today in the office for primary hypertension. Her medications were reviewed and scripts were written. Impacting her status, it should be noted that she has a history of tobacco dependence.
ICD-10-CM code(s): _____

20. The 25-year-old patient took Percodan as prescribed and now presents to the office due to extreme nausea. It is determined that he is having an adverse effect of Percodan.
ICD-10-CM code(s): _____

21. The patient is seen in the physician's office for a follow-up after suffering an anterolateral ST elevation myocardial infarction 4 weeks ago. The patient is also evaluated for Type 1 diabetes mellitus with associated polyneuropathy.
ICD-10-CM code(s): _____

22. The 45-year-old male was seen in the ambulatory surgery center for tubular adenoma of the rectum. The surgeon performs a colonoscopy and excision of the adenoma.
ICD-10-CM code(s): _____

ICD-10-PCS code(s): _____

23. The 54-year-old female is admitted with carcinoma of the lower-outer quadrant of the left breast. The surgeon performs a radical mastectomy.
ICD-10-CM code(s): _____

ICD-10-PCS code(s): _____

24. A 62-year-old male was seen in the emergency department for chest pain. He has been previously diagnosed with atherosclerotic heart disease and has a history of hypertension that is treated with medication. No history of surgical procedures. ED physician documents the following diagnosis:

ASHD with unstable angina

Hypertension

ICD-10-CM code(s): _____

25. The 19-year-old patient was seen in the physician's office for nausea as a result of accidentally taking too much Robitussin (dextromethorphan) for a cough.

ICD-10-CM code(s): _____

26. The patient's diagnosis was confirmed as carcinoma of the right ovary with metastasis to the omentum.

ICD-10-CM code(s): _____

27. Patient is seen in the clinic for a change of tracheostomy tube.

ICD-10-CM code(s): _____

ICD-10-PCS code(s): _____

28. Patient suffered a traumatic displaced, cervical (C2) fracture.

ICD-10-CM code(s): _____

29. A 28-year-old female, 38 weeks gestation, with maternal hypotension delivers a liveborn male infant. Normal spontaneous vaginal delivery.

ICD-10-CM code(s): _____

ICD-10-PCS code(s): _____

30. Patient seen in the Emergency Department for leakage of prosthetic heart valve.

ICD-10-CM code(s): _____

Decision-Based Coding

This chapter will focus on the skill of decision-based coding. The case study exercises have been assigned ICD-10-CM diagnosis and ICD-10-PCS procedure codes. The decision-based coding process requires the coding professional to defend the code selection based on integrated knowledge and the supportive documentation that tells the patient's clinical story. This task involves a change to the traditional coding workflow process of producing a code. This change requires analysis of coded data to *support* or *not support* the selected code assignment. These skills can be applied to the auditing function as well as in the role of clinical code editor in the world of computer-assisted coding (CAC).

Computer-Assisted Coding (CAC)

For many years, software vendors have developed technological solutions to assist with coding. In addition to encoders, editing tools, and searchable database of resources, the next generation of technological tools is being introduced to the industry: CAC. CAC software involves a complicated logic technological process that relies on systems such as national language processing or structured text input.

With CAC, coders will be asked to *accept or not accept* the computer-generated codes based on analysis of the patient's clinical story documented in the health record and application of all the knowledge and skill required of clinical coders. Coding professionals need to base their decisions on a combined knowledge of disease processes, coding principles, and clinical concepts. The clinical editor role must recognize inconsistencies and inappropriate application of coding guidelines.

Case Study Exercises

The intent of this exercise is to apply all of the knowledge and skills to support or reject the codes that have been assigned. Many facilities plan to use ICD-10-PCS for data collection for outpatient surgery cases. For that reason, the case studies were selected from both the inpatient and outpatient settings.

Read the following case studies to assimilate the patient's clinical picture. Reference the listed ICD-10-CM and ICD-10-PCS codes and compare this assignment to the documentation. Validate the coding selection and in the "Rationale" section of the table, document what key points drove your decision. If the code is incorrect, assign the correct code and note the difference. Code only procedures found in the Medical-Surgical Section of ICD-10-PCS.

Answers to case studies 1–5 are located in Appendix A, and the remaining answers are provided only to educators through the instructor online companion.

Case Study 1

OPERATIVE REPORT

PREOPERATIVE DIAGNOSIS: Left hip mass

POSTOPERATIVE DIAGNOSIS: Hemangioma, left hip

OPERATIVE PROCEDURE: Excision of mass from hip

ANESTHESIA: General endotracheal anesthesia

INDICATIONS: This 1-year-old child presents with a mass on her left hip area, which is soft, moveable, and in the subcutaneous tissue.

DESCRIPTION OF PROCEDURE: Under satisfactory general anesthesia, the patient was placed in the supine position. The abdomen and left hip were prepped with Betadine gel and draped in a routine fashion. Marcaine was injected over the mass just below her birthmark and the previously marked incision. The incision was made with a scalpel and dissection carried through the superficial fascia with the cautery. The underlying 0.6-cm mass was then slowly dissected free from the surrounding subcutaneous fibrofatty tissue. It had several small vessels feeding it, which were cauterized. There were several lobules of small tufts of vascular tissue, suggesting a hemangioma. They tended to insinuate in fingers in the subcutaneous tissue in various directions. These were all gently dissected free superiorly toward the iliac crest and inferiorly, medially, and laterally. The supplying vessels were doubly clamped, divided, and ligated with 3-0 Vicryl suture. A No. 10 Blake drain was placed into the cavity after assuring hemostasis and irrigating it with saline. It was brought out through a separate skin incision and secured to the skin with 4-0 nylon. Specimen was sent to pathology for confirmed diagnosis.

The subcutaneous tissue was reapproximated with an interrupted 5-0 undyed Vicryl suture and the skin was closed with Steri-Strips. Sterile dressings were placed on the wounds and the patient, having tolerated the procedure well, was returned to the recovery room in satisfactory condition with vital signs stable.

Coding Assignment	Rationale
ICD-10-CM Code(s): D18.01 Hemangioma of skin and subcutaneous tissue	
ICD-10-PCS Code(s): 0JBL0ZZ Excision of Right Upper Leg Subcutaneous Tissue and Fascia, Open Approach	

Case Study 2

OPERATIVE REPORT

PREOPERATIVE DIAGNOSIS: Biliary colic

POSTOPERATIVE DIAGNOSIS: Biliary colic

PROCEDURE PERFORMED: Laparoscopic cholecystectomy

FINDINGS: The patient had normal anatomy. The cystic duct was small; therefore, a cholangiogram catheter could not be introduced into the duct.

DESCRIPTION OF THE PROCEDURE: The patient was taken to the operating room and placed in the supine position. The patient was prepped and draped in the usual sterile manner. Endotracheal anesthesia was administered.

An infraumbilical incision was made and the abdomen was entered using the open Hasson technique. The abdomen was insufflated with CO_2 without difficulty. The laparoscope was inserted and no injuries were identified. An 11-mm VersaStep trocar was placed in the mid-epigastric region and two 5-mm trocars were placed in the right lateral abdomen. These were all placed under direct visualization of the laparoscope. The cystic duct was bluntly dissected out. A clip was placed proximally on the gallbladder and a ductotomy was performed. The patient had a very small cystic duct. This would not allow introduction of the cholangiocatheter. The cystic duct was then doubly clipped and transected. The cystic artery was doubly clipped and transected. The gallbladder was then removed from the liver bed using the Hook laser cautery. There was no spillage of stones or bile. The gallbladder was placed in an Endobag and removed through the infraumbilical port site. The liver bed was inspected and hemostasis was achieved. The trocars were removed under visualization of the laparoscope. The infraumbilical fascia was approximated with 0 Vicryl in an interrupted fashion. The skin was closed with 4-0 Caprosyn in a running subcuticular fashion. The wounds were infiltrated with 0.5% Marcaine with epinephrine. The patient had Steri-Strips and a sterile dressing was applied.

The patient was taken to recovery with no apparent intraoperative complications.

Coding Assignment	Rationale
ICD-10-CM Code(s): K80.50 Calculus of bile duct without cholangitis or cholecystitis without obstruction	
ICD-10-PCS Code(s): 0FT44ZZ Resection of Gallbladder, Percutaneous Endoscopic Approach	

Case Study 3

OPERATIVE REPORT

PREOPERATIVE DIAGNOSIS: Retained hardware right tibia

POSTOPERATIVE DIAGNOSIS: Retained hardware right tibia

PROCEDURE: Hardware removal right tibia

INDICATIONS: This 16-year-old male previously underwent an intramedullary nailing of his right tibial shaft fracture. His tibia has healed and he now is seeking removal of the hardware.

DESCRIPTION OF PROCEDURE: Under general anesthesia and tourniquet control, the patient's right leg was prepped and draped using normal sterile technique. The previous incisions were used to approach the proximal and distal screw holes. The proximal screw was approached first. Next, the distal screw was approached and it was easily identifiable and it was removed without difficulty. Dissection proximally was tedious, and the proximal screw was not readily apparent. Image intensification was used to approach the proximal screw. The lateral portion of the proximal screw was palpated percutaneously and the end was identified. This was used as a marker. A single drill hole was made in the tibia and the screw head was identified slightly anterior to the drill hole itself. The vast majority of the screw head was overgrown with bone. The overgrown bone was removed without difficulty. The screw was backed out. Next, image intensifier was used to approach the proximal end of the rod. The proximal end was identified, and bone was cleared away from the proximal end of the rod. This bone also invaded the screw cap. The bone was removed from the screw cap, and the screw cap was removed. In order to place the inserter/extractor bolt, the proximal rod had to be drilled to remove bone from the center portion of the rod. Once the bone was drilled, the inserter extractor screw was tightened. The tuning fork hammer was used to remove the rod. This was done once the rod had broken free from the bone nearby. All hardware was removed to be sterilized and given to the patient. The wounds were copiously irrigated and closed with absorbable sutures on the subcutaneous tissues, and the skin was closed with staples. Marcaine was instilled and a light dressing was placed at the knee and ankle.

TOURNIQUET TIME: 85 minutes.

BLOOD LOSS: Minimal.

COMPLICATIONS: None.

PLAN: The patient was given a prescription for 30 mg Vicodin for postoperative pain control. He will return to see me in the office in a week for dressing removal and a week later for removal of all staples. Next week we can remove some of the staples. We should also get an X-ray of his right tibia, two views, at that time.

Coding Assignment	Rationale
ICD-10-CM Code(s): S82.201A Unspecified fracture of shaft of right tibia	
ICD-10-PCS Code(s): 0QPGX4Z Removal of Internal Fixation Device from Right Tibia, External Approach	

Case Study 4

OUTPATIENT SURGERY CENTER

PROCEDURE PERFORMED: Esophagogastroduodenoscopy (EGD) with biopsy

INSTRUMENT USED: Olympus GAF-160 upper video endoscope

MEDICATIONS ADMINISTERED: Fentanyl 150 mcg intravenously, Versed 3 mg intravenously, and Hurricaine spray topically.

INDICATION: Dysphagia

HISTORY: Patient has had a history of difficulty when swallowing. Conservation treatment has failed, and diagnostic/surgical intervention was recommended.

DESCRIPTION OF PROCEDURE: The patient was brought to the outpatient operative suite and placed in left lateral decubitus position. His throat was anesthetized with Hurricaine spray. Conscious sedation was induced and maintained with the intravenous medications listed earlier.

The endoscope was passed by direct vision into the oropharynx and upper esophagus and then advanced carefully and without difficulty under direct vision to a depth of the proximal small bowel. Retroflexion of the scope was performed in the stomach, with a clear view of the fundus and cardia obtained.

FINDINGS: The esophagus showed some irregularity to the Z line. It was difficult to tell exactly where the esophagus ended and the stomach began. A biopsy was taken from the distal esophagus to rule out Barrett's esophagus. There were no ulcerations or erosions. There were no strictures or rings. The scope passed easily into the gastric remnant. No lesions were seen within the gastric remnant. The first portion of the small bowel was then explored for several centimeters and no lesions were seen. He tolerated the procedure well and without apparent immediate complication.

IMPRESSION: Dysphagia.

Long-standing gastroesophageal reflux disease (GERD), rule out Barrett's esophagus.

RECOMMENDATION: We will await the patient's biopsy results regarding Barrett's esophagus.

Coding Assignment	Rationale
ICD-10-CM Code(s): R13.10 Dysphagia, unspecified K21.9 Gastro-esophageal reflux disease without esophagitis K22.70 Barrett's esophagus without dysplasia	
ICD-10-PCS Code(s): 0DB38ZZ Excision of Lower Esophagus, Via Natural or Artificial Opening Endoscopic	

Case Study 5

OUTPATIENT SURGERY DEPARTMENT

PROGRESS NOTE: Patient has cardiac arrhythmia. The patient's loop recorder currently is at end-of-life. The patient comes now for removal of the cardiac event recorder device.

OPERATIVE NOTE: The patient has no known allergies. She received 1 g of Ancef intravenously periprocedurally. The left periclavicular area, the location of the device, was prepped and draped in the usual fashion. Using local anesthetic was administered lidocaine without epinephrine. The wound was opened and sutures that were holding the device were removed. The device was removed and the wound was cleaned with Betadine swabs. Subsequently, saline was used to remove the Betadine. Hemostasis was achieved without needing cautery. The wound was closed in two layers. The first layer was 3-0 interrupted Vicryl. The second layer was 4-0 interrupted Vicryl subcuticular. The patient tolerated the procedure well. There was no immediate complication.

Coding Assignment	Rationale
ICD-10-CM Code(s): Z45.09 Encounter for adjustment and management of other cardiac device I49.9 Cardiac arrhythmia, unspecified	
ICD-10-PCS Code(s): 0WP80YZ Removal of Other Device from Chest Wall, Open Approach	

Case Study 6

OUTPATIENT SURGERY DEPARTMENT

PREOPERATIVE PROGRESS NOTE: This 35-year-old patient, Gravida 5, Para 4, AB 0, desires sterilization. The consequences and risks have been explained to the patient.

OPERATIVE REPORT

PREOPERATIVE DIAGNOSIS: Desires permanent sterilization

POSTOPERATIVE DIAGNOSIS: Desires permanent sterilization

OPERATION PERFORMED: Laparoscopic bilateral tubal sterilization using bipolar cautery

ANESTHESIA: General

FINDINGS: The uterus, ovaries, and fallopian tubes were normal in size and appearance.

PROCEDURE: In the operating room general anesthesia was administered and the patient was positioned into low lithotomy with feet apart in Allen stirrups. She was sterilely prepped and draped for laparoscopy. Foley catheter was placed. The HUMI catheter was inserted into the uterus. A small vertical subumbilical incision was made with the scalpel in the abdomen and centered in an open laparoscopy fashion. A 10-mm Hasson trocar was inserted bluntly through the subumbilical incision in the usual fashion and secured with 0 Polysorb suture previously placed in the fascia on either side of the trocar. The abdomen was insufflated with CO_2 gas to a pressure of 15 PSI. Pelvis was examined. A small suprapubic incision was made with a scalpel and the 5-mm trocar was inserted under direct visualization. Starting on the left side, 3 to 4 cm of fallopian tube was cauterized with bipolar cautery until disconnected. This was done on the right side in the same fashion. Hemostasis was excellent. Then all instrumentation was removed from the abdominal wall, and the gas was expelled from the abdominal cavity. The fascia below the subumbilical incision was approximated with uninterrupted 0 Polysorb figure-of-eight suture. The subumbilical skin incision was closed with 3-0 Polysorb running subcuticular suture. The lower abdominal incision was approximated with Steri-Strips and benzoin on the skin. Both skin incisions were infiltrated with 0.5% Marcaine with epinephrine 1:2,000 and dressings were applied. She was cleaned and undraped. She was awakened from anesthesia. Patient was transferred to a gurney and taken to recovery in satisfactory condition.

ESTIMATED BLOOD LOSS: Minimal.

SPECIMENS: Cauterized segments of right and left fallopian tubes.

DRAINS AND PACKS: Foley catheter was removed in the operating room just prior to leaving for PACU.

NEEDLE AND SPONGE COUNT: Reported as correct.

PROGNOSIS: Immediate and remote are both good.

COMPLICATIONS: None.

Coding Assignment	Rationale
ICD-10-CM Code(s): Z30.2 Encounter for sterilization	
ICD-10-PCS Code(s): 0UB74ZZ Excision of Bilateral Fallopian Tubes, Percutaneous Endoscopic Approach	

Case Study 7

OPERATIVE REPORT

PREOPERATIVE DIAGNOSIS: Comminuted right closed mid shaft clavicle fracture

POSTOPERATIVE DIAGNOSIS: Comminuted right closed mid shaft clavicle fracture

PROCEDURE: Open reduction internal fixation right clavicle

ANESTHESIA: General

DESCRIPTION OF PROCEDURE: After providing informed consent, Levi was brought to the operating room whereupon smooth induction of general anesthesia was performed, the patient was positioned in a beach chair position on the operating room table, and all bony prominences were well padded. A bump was placed under the proximal thoracic spine to allow the scapula and shoulder to retract on the right. The right upper extremity was prepped and draped in the standard sterile fashion from the neck to the midline of the chest to the fingertips. An alcohol pre-prep was used. The clavicle fracture was readily palpable about the mid shaft. A longitudinal incision overlying the subcutaneous border of the clavicle centered on the deformity was made and length was approximately 10 cm. The skin and subcutaneous tissue were carefully dissected sharply down to the level of the periosteum overlying the clavicle. Hemostasis was carefully obtained using Bovie cautery. The clavicle fracture was dissected free of early soft callus in a subperiosteal fashion superiorly and anteriorly. The medial and lateral fragments were identified. The central comminution was noted to be severe with at least three fragments making up the central area in addition to the larger medial and lateral fragments. The fracture margins were carefully cleaned using suction, a small rongeur, and a small curet. Following this, a careful anatomic reduction was obtained manually and held using multiple bony reduction clamps. Care was taken throughout the operation to protect the subclavian vessels about the inferior surface of the clavicle.

Once the provisional reduction had been achieved and was maintained with bone clamps, two interfragmentary lag screws from the Acumed precontoured clavicle plate set (titanium) were used to hold the provisional reduction and this was successful. An eight-hold right-sided precontoured clavicle titanium plate was then removed from the set and placed over the fracture. The right-sided plate was at the least bend was found to fit well. However, it fit better in a reverse position with the intended medial end facing laterally. This was because the fracture encompassed more of the lateral bend of the clavicle as opposed to the medial bend. The plate required some contouring medially and this was done with plate benders. The plate was then solidly fixed to the bone in a noncompression fashion using 3.5-mm fully threaded cortical titanium screws from the set. All eight holes were filled. Three lateral screws and two medial screws were fully in the lateral and medial fragments, respectively. The three central screws were attached to portions of the lateral and medial fragments as well as the intervening comminution. Screw length was checked by direct palpations and intraoperatively using a flat plate X-ray. The reduction of the fracture and position of the hardware was confirmed and the wound was copiously irrigated with normal saline. It was then closed in layers using 0 Vicryl suture in a simple interrupted fashion for the deep fascia. The subcutaneous tissue was closed using interrupted 3-0 Monocryl suture in a simple buried fashion. A subcuticular 4-0 Prolene suture was then used to close skin. Steri-Strips and a sterile compressive dressing were applied and the patient was placed in a right upper extremity sling. He was awakened from anesthesia and taken to the recovery room in stable condition. Estimated blood loss was 250 mL. There were no intraoperative complications. Postoperatively he will be strictly non–weight bearing on the right upper extremity with use of a sling. He will have PO pain medicine for pain control. If he requires admission for pain control, I expect this to be less than 24 hours.

Coding Assignment	Rationale
ICD-10-CM Code(s): S42.021A Displaced fracture of shaft of right clavicle	
ICD-10-PCS Code(s): 0PSB34Z Reposition Left Clavicle with Internal Fixation Device, Percutaneous Approach	

Case Study 8

OPERATIVE REPORT

PREOPERATIVE DIAGNOSIS: Left breast lump, large 2+ cm

POSTOPERATIVE DIAGNOSIS: Left breast lump, large 2+ cm

PROCEDURE PERFORMED: Left breast lumpectomy through a circumareolar incision

ANESTHESIA: General

COMPLICATIONS: None

DESCRIPTION OF PROCEDURE: The patient was placed in the supine position, and the breast was prepped and draped. A marking pen was used to mark the line of incision, which was from about 12 o'clock to the 3 o'clock position in the circumareolar area. The incision was made, the skin was raised with skin hooks, and using sharp and blunt dissection I was able to dissect all the way to the palpable lump. A lumpectomy was performed, removing the lump in toto, not cutting into the lesion at all. Hemostasis was then achieved by electrocautery. The wound was then closed with 3-0 Vicryl suture and subcuticular 4-0 Monocryl suture and Steri-Strips. There were no problems or complications. The patient left the OR in good condition.

Coding Assignment	Rationale
ICD-10-CM Code(s): N63 Lump in breast	
ICD-10-PCS Code(s): 0HBU0ZX Excision of Left Breast, Open Approach, Diagnostic	

Case Study 9

OPERATIVE REPORT

PREOPERATIVE DIAGNOSIS: Primary osteoarthritis of the right knee

POSTOPERATIVE DIAGNOSIS: Primary osteoarthritis of the right knee

PROCEDURE: Right posterior stabilized total knee arthroplasty

ANESTHESIA: General plus right femoral block

IMPLANTS: DePuy Sigma System size 4 right posterior stabilized femoral component, size 3 modular tibial tray with 8 mm non-crosslinked polyethylene spacer, and 35 mm × 8.5 mm thick patella. Antibiotic cement was used.

PROCEDURE IN DETAIL: The patient was brought to the OR and positioned in supine fashion with all bony prominences well padded. A bump was placed under the right hip, and a tourniquet was placed on the right proximal thigh. A gram of Kefzol was given intravenously. The right lower extremity was prepped and draped in standard sterile fashion for arthroplasty, including an alcohol pre-prep.

After exsanguination of the extremity with an Ace wrap, the tourniquet was inflated to 300 mmHg. An approximately 6-inch longitudinal incision was made about the anterior aspect of the knee centered on the inferior pole of the patella. The skin and subcutaneous tissue were dissected sharply down to the level of the fascia, and a medial parapatellar incision was made in the fascia with the medial most split proximally. The patella was everted, and the knee was flexed. Care was taken to protect the patellar tendon insertion. The osteophytes about the femoral notch were removed, and a partial resection of the posterior patellar fat pad was carried out. No significant medial release was carried out because of the valgus deformity of the knee. The femoral canal was entered with a drill, and the sword with distal femoral cutting guide was attached set for a resection of 10 mm at 6 degrees of valgus. The lateral femoral condyle was noted to be eroded distally and posteriorly. However, a 10-mm cut was sufficient for the distal cut.

Using anterior-referenced system, the femur was sized to a size 4. Rotation was set at 3 degrees external rotation. This was checked using the epicondylar axis. The four-in-one cutting guide was then applied, and the distal femoral anterior and posterior cuts as well as chamfer cuts were completed. This went well. Care was taken to protect the collateral ligaments during these cuts. The femoral notch was then completed using the notch-cutting guide supplied with the system. Once this was done, attention was turned to the tibia. Using an external referenced guide, a tibial cut was made with a zero degree posterior slope with 2 mm off the low (lateral) side. This resection resulted in a similar amount of resection medially and laterally. The tibia was exposed using a Homan placed posteriorly and laterally. The osteophytes were removed laterally and posteriorly.

At this point the osteophytes about the posterior femoral condyles were removed using a curved osteotome under direct visualization. Care was taken to protect the posterior structures. The tibia was then sized to a size 3. A thin cut was then made for the modular tibial tray system. An 8-mm posterior stabilized trial spacer, size 3 tibial tray, and size 4 femur were then applied. The knee was taken through a range of motion, and there was a tightness noted laterally. The lateral collateral ligament was recessed slightly off the lateral femoral condyle. Following this, stability was symmetric medially and laterally. The patella was then prepared. The osteophytes were removed with a rongeur, and the thickness was measured to be 25 mm. An 8.5-mm resection was made down to 16.5 mm, and a 16.5 × 35 mm patellar trial was applied after the cut was completed. Stability of this component was then trialed, and it was found to be excellent.

The trial components were removed, and the knee was copiously irrigated with normal saline. The final components were then cemented in place in the sizes mentioned earlier. Order of cement was patella, tibia, femur. The tibial tray was placed and the knee brought out into full extension to compress the tibial and femoral components. Again, antibiotic gentamicin-containing cement was used. The wound was then cleared of excess cement and bony debris and irrigated one final time. It was then closed in layers over a ConstaVac drain. Number 1 Vicryl was used for the extensor fascia and Scarpa fascia in a simple interrupted fashion, 3-0 Monocryl was used for the subcutaneous tissue in a simple buried fashion, and staples were placed at the level of the skin.

A sterile dressing was placed. The ConstaVac drain extension and reservoir were attached and activated, and a compressive wrap was placed from the toes to the thigh. The tourniquet was released for a total tourniquet time of 112 minutes. EBL was minimal. There were no intra-operative complications. Postoperatively the patient was taken to the recovery room in stable condition. She will begin CPM today. She will begin weightbearing as tolerated with physical therapy on postoperative day 1. ConstaVac, Foley, PCA, and antibiotics will be used for 24 to 48 hours. DVT prophylaxis will be with Coumadin and foot pumps.

Coding Assignment	Rationale
ICD-10-CM Code(s): M17.11 Osteoarthritis of knee	
ICD-10-PCS Code(s): 0SRC0JA Replacement of Right Knee Joint with Synthetic Substitute, Uncemented, Open Approach	

Case Study 10

DIAGNOSIS: Deep Vein Thrombosis-legs

PROCEDURE: Inferior vena cava filter placement

DESCRIPTION OF THE PROCEDURE: The patient was taken to the cath lab, placed in supine position, and prepped and draped in a routine manner. Right femoral vein access was obtained guided by the venacavagram. The filter was then advanced under fluoroscopic guidance and deployed at the L1-L2 interspace. It appeared to be fully expanded and stable in position. The introducer sheath was withdrawn. A single 4-0 Vicryl suture was placed in the groin skin. Pressure was applied to the right groin access site for 5 minutes. At this point, the wound appeared to be hemostatic. Dressings were applied. The patient was then returned to the ward appearing to have tolerated the procedure well.

Coding Assignment	Rationale
ICD-10-CM Code(s): I80.209 Thrombosis	
ICD-10-PCS Code(s): 06H00DZ Insertion of Intraluminal Device into Inferior Vena Cava, Open Approach	

Case Study 11

OPERATIVE REPORT

PREOPERATIVE DIAGNOSIS: Small distal left ureteral calculus

POSTOPERATIVE DIAGNOSIS: Small distal left ureteral calculus

PROCEDURE: Cystoscopy with left ureteroscopy and extraction of ureteral calculus

ANESTHESIA: General

SUMMARY: The patient's preoperative KUB was difficult to interpret and I could not be certain of the location of the patient's stone. He specifically stated that he had strained all of his urine since I saw him in the office yesterday, at which time I confirmed the presence of his distal left ureteral stone radiographically, and he found no stone in his strainer. He had, however, had a fairly comfortable night.

The patient was brought to the operating room and placed supine on the lithotripsy table and a general anesthesia was induced. Fluoroscopic imaging with the C-arm failed to confirm the presence of his stone reliably. Accordingly, the patient was brought down to the bottom of the lithotripsy table and placed in the lithotomy position. His genitalia were then sterilely prepped and draped and a 24 French cystourethroscope was advanced under direct vision toward the urinary bladder. In the very proximal urethra, I suddenly encountered the patient's stone, which had obviously passed into the bladder and then through the bladder neck at some point following the patient's last urination. This stone proved to be rather flat but an obvious calcium oxalate dihydrate stone of about the dimensions noted on the patient's CT scan and yellow-brown in coloration with a very rough surface.

A flexible alligator grasping forceps was therefore used through the working channel of the cystoscope and this was employed to grasp the stone and extract it completely. The stone was then sent to pathology for chemical analysis.

In order to be certain that this represented the only stone this patient had, a semi-rigid uretero-scope was passed under direct vision into the bladder and the left ureteral orifice was carefully evaluated. It was noted to be mildly edematous and erythematous but open. I was able to pass the ureteroscope through the intramural ureter and found no evidence of residual stones but the ureteral mucosa in the intramural ureter was definitely traumatized, as would be expected if the patient had recently passed a stone through that area.

I therefore concluded that the stone extracted represented this patient's presenting problem and the procedure was terminated.

The patient tolerated the procedure well and was sent to recovery in satisfactory and stable condition.

Coding Assignment	Rationale
ICD-10-CM Code(s): N20.1 Calculus of ureter	
ICD-10-PCS Code(s): 0TCD8ZZ Extirpation of Matter from Urethra, Via Natural or Artificial Opening Endoscopic	

Case Study 12

OPERATIVE REPORT

PREOPERATIVE DIAGNOSIS: Bilateral subdural hematoma

POSTOPERATIVE DIAGNOSIS: Bilateral subdural hematoma

PROCEDURE: Bilateral bur-hole craniotomies with drain insertion

FINDINGS: As above.

ESTIMATED BLOOD LOSS: 100 mL

SPECIMENS: Subdural fluid.

SPONGE AND NEEDLE COUNTS: Sponge and needle counts were appropriate.

HISTORY: The patient was in the hospital with weakness and sense of balance problems ever since she had a fall approximately 4 weeks ago where she split her head open and had stitches. Following that, she had difficulty with a sense of generalized weakness and balance problems. She was brought to the hospital when this persisted. In the hospital a CT scan of the head showing bilateral subdural hematomas was obtained; therefore, neurosurgery was consulted. It was determined that the patient could benefit from surgical intervention. After informed consent, surgery was planned.

DESCRIPTION OF PROCEDURE: The patient was brought to the operative suite where she was anesthetized and intubated on a hospital operative table in the supine position. She was then appropriately padded and positioned, and then sterilely prepped and draped in the usual fashion. This was done only after shaving hair over the areas to be incised. Once this had been done, a small, approximately 3 cm, incision was made in the area, approximately 2 cm cephalad to the pinna of the ear and approximately 3 cm anterior to the anterior most portion of the ear. The incision was made with a #10 scalpel after using approximately 4 mL of 0.25% preserve-free Marcaine. The skin was incised and carried down to the skull. All points of bleeding were controlled with unipolar cautery. Exposure of the skull was provided with a small Weitlaner. Once the skull was cleared of any soft tissue, then a perforator drill was brought into the field and bur-hole craniotomy was performed. Once this trepanation had been accomplished, then the bony remnants were removed with Kerrison rongeur. Then, using a bipolar cautery, a cruciate mark was made on the dura, and then the dura was opened with a #11 blade.

The subdural fluid collection then was drained, first on the right side. It was flushed with fluid, and there were no signs of any active bleeding. When the fluid had been removed and was no longer draining, then a round 10-French drain was placed. Once this was in place, then a small stab incision, approximately 3 cm, posterior to the incision was then made and a hemostat was used to create a path and bring the drain out through the skin. The drain was then secured with #0 Nurolon, and then the skin was closed in 2 layers, first the galeal layer was reapproximated with #0 Nurolon in an interrupted fashion, and then the skin was closed with staples. Once this was done, the same procedure was performed on the left side. When both sides had been completed, then povidone gel was used over the staples and over the stab incision for the drain. The skin was cleaned prior to that, and then a 4 × 4 was placed over each side with an OpSite dressing over each.

The patient was then removed from the operative table in satisfactory condition and taken to the recovery room.

Coding Assignment	Rationale
ICD-10-CM Code(s): S06.6X0A Traumatic subarachnoid hemorrhage without loss of consciousness, initial encounter	
ICD-10-PCS Code(s): 00940ZX Drainage of Subdural Space, Open Approach, Diagnostic	

Case Study 13

OPERATIVE REPORT

DIAGNOSIS: Carcinoma of the lung

PROCEDURE: Fiberoptic bronchoscopy

Indications for Procedure: Lung mass

TECHNIQUE: The patient was brought to the Cardiopulmonary Department and after obtaining an IV and preparing his airways with topical lidocaine, the patient was sedated with initially 2 mg of Versed and 2 mg of morphine, and an additional 2 mg of Versed was given through the procedure because of coughing and some respiratory difficulty after insertion of the broncho-scope. The scope was advanced into the nares without difficulty. The epiglottis was normal. The larynx was irregular with white friable lesions but no malignant appearing lesions. The cords moved normally with phonation. Lidocaine was instilled into the cords and the scope was advanced into the airway without difficulty. The patient did have some coughing through the procedure. Lidocaine was instilled into the trachea, carina and pooling of lidocaine was noted in the right mainstem bronchus. The lidocaine was suctioned from the right mainstem bronchus and this revealed a complete obstruction with an endobronchial tumor of the right mainstem bronchus approximately 2 cm from the carina. The left mainstem was normal. Left upper lobe, lingual, and lower lobe basilar segments were within normal limits. The scope was returned to the right mainstem bronchus and multiple endobronchial biopsies were performed. Bronchial washings were collected and a cytology brush was advanced to prepare slides and cytology brushings for cytopathology. The scope was removed without difficulty. The patient tolerated the procedure well.

Coding Assignment	Rationale
ICD-10-CM Code(s): C34.90 Malignant neoplasm of unspecified part of unspecified bronchus or lung	
ICD-10-PCS Code(s): 0BB37ZX Excision of Right Main Bronchus, Via Natural or Artificial Opening, Diagnostic	

Case Study 14

OPERATIVE REPORT

PREOPERATIVE DIAGNOSIS: Perforated diverticulitis at the sigmoid colon

POSTOPERATIVE DIAGNOSIS: Perforated diverticulitis at the sigmoid colon

PROCEDURE: Laparoscopic sigmoid colon resection with end descending colostomy

TECHNIQUE: The patient was brought to the operative suite and placed in supine position. After obtaining adequate general endotracheal anesthesia, the abdomen was prepped and draped in the usual sterile fashion. The abdomen was accessed through a supraumbilical transrectus Endopath trocar technique, and a 5-mm trocar was placed without difficulty. Another 5-mm trocar was placed subxiphoid, and a 12-mm trocar was placed in the right lower quadrant. Diverticulitis was identified in the pelvis with free perforation as described. This was about the mid sigmoid colon. There was a fair amount of redundancy. There was a decent amount of health colon distal to the diseased area. That was divided with a 60-mm blue load GIA stapler. Three loads of white load stapler were fired on the mesentery to create some laxity in the mesentery. The colon was then delivered through a left abdominal wall defect created for ostomy through the rectus muscle. The defect needed to be larger than normal for a colostomy just because of the immense size of the diseased sigmoid colon. That fascial opening was then closed down with some 0 PCS suture at the conclusion to snugly close around the descending colon at the ostomy. Surgical sites were all evaluated. Irrigation of the abdominal space ensued with a good clean space left remaining. All the irrigant was aspirated. Bowel was placed back in what was hoped to be a nonobstructive pattern. The trocar sites were closed with subcuticular Vicryl suture and covered with Dermabond. The colon was then divided outside the abdomen with cautery. The mesentery ligated as appropriate with Vicryl ties. The ostomy was then matured in the typical fashion with 3-0 Vicryl suture. It was technically very satisfactory and a well-perfused piece of colon was noted at the ostomy. The patient was being prepared for awakening and extubated at the time of dictation. She tolerated the procedure well.

Coding Assignment	Rationale
ICD-10-CM Code(s): K57.20 Diverticulitis of large intestine with perforation and abscess without bleeding	
ICD-10-PCS Code(s): 0D1M8ZN Bypass Descending Colon to Sigmoid Colon, Via Natural or Artificial Opening Endoscopic	

Case 15

OPERATIVE REPORT

DIAGNOSIS: Aortic valve Stenosis

PROCEDURE: Aortic valve replacement utilizing a 21 mm St. Jude Medical® Regent™ synthetic prosthesis, serial #2773399

INDICATIONS: This is a 77-year-old female who has been having chest pressure with exertion as well as shortness of breath. Workup showed severe aortic valve stenosis with a peak velocity of 4.73 and a gradient of 89 mmHg. Based on the patient symptomatology as well as objective findings, she was referred for valve replacement.

DETAILS OF PROCEDURE: After obtaining informed consent, the patient was taken to the operating room and placed supine upon the OR table. Antibiotics were initiated and the patient was smoothly induced into general anesthesia, and all appropriate cardiac lines as well as the echo probe were placed. Timeout was performed confirming patient name, date of birth, allergies, and surgical procedure. The neck, chest, abdomen, groin, and legs were then prepped with alcohol and DuraPrep solution followed by placement of sterile towels and drapes to create a surgical border. A standard sternotomy incision was then made and the pericardium was opened longitudinally and T-d at the diaphragm. We then heparinized the patient and fashioned a pericardial well. The aorta and pulmonary artery were separated and then the aorta was cannulated with a 7-mm Sarns Soft Flow cannula with a 37 two-stage line placed to the right atrial appendage. Antegrade and retrograde myocardial protection catheters were then inserted, and the patient was taken on bypass and decompressed at which time we placed a left ventricular vent through the right superior pulmonary vein. The patient was then cooled and we cross-clamped the aorta and arrested the heart with oxygenated cold blood cardioplegia. A transverse aortotomy incision was then made and angled toward the mid aspect of the noncoronary cusp. Retraction sutures were placed and the valve was excised. We then copiously irrigated the aortic root and left ventricular outflow tract with iced saline solution and then sized to 21-mm prosthesis. Nonpledgeted 1-0 Tycron was then placed in simple fashion around the annulus and we then sutured in the valve, finding it to seat appropriately. We then reirrigated the aortic valve with iced saline solution and then closed the aorta in two layers with pledgeted 4-0 Prolene.

At this point, the patient had been re-warmed and we placed her in steep Trendelenburg position. The heart was filled with blood and the lungs ventilated, all while performing standard de-airing procedures. Once we were happy there was no residual intracardiac air, the aortic cross-clamp and retrograde catheter were removed. The heart spontaneously entered a sinus bradycardia. We did place atrial and ventricular pacemaker wires and AV paced at 90 bets per minute. Echo was then re-performed showing no evidence of perivalvular leak. We were happy there was no residual intracardiac air and at this point could remove the left ventricular vent. We then separated from bypass without difficulty and the venous line was taken out as was the root-vent catheter. The venous line was removed and all pump blood was reinfused through the aortic cannula during protamine administration. The aortic line was taken out and all cannulation sites were hemostatic. Anterior and posterior mediastinal tubes were placed as was a pleural tube directed in the left side. The pericardium was then interrupted closed and the sternum approximated with #5 stainless steel wire. The linea alba was closed with an interrupted 1 Vicryl, and a 1 Vicryl was used to close the pectoralis major fascia. 2-0 Vicryl was used in the subcutaneous fat and skin was closed with a subdermal Vicryl. A sterile dressing was applied and the patient transferred to ICU. Sponge, needle, and instrument counts were reported correct × 2.

Coding Assignment	Rationale
ICD-10-CM Code(s): I35.0 Nonrheumatic aortic valve stenosis	
ICD-10-PCS Code(s): 02RF0KZ Replacement of Aortic Valve with Nonautologous Tissue Substitute, Open Approach	

Appendix A: Answer Key

Answers for Chapter 1: Infectious and Parasitic Diseases

Check Your Knowledge of Infectious Diseases

Column A	Column B
1. __B__ bacterial organism	A. histoplasmosis
2. __D__ viral infection	B. *staphylococcus*
3. __A__ fungal infection	C. malaria
4. __C__ protozoal disease	D. herpes zoster

Check Your Clinical Knowledge

1. **Pneumococcal pneumonia** is the most common infectious disease complication of both measles and influenza. *Clostridium difficile* (called *C. diff*) is a bacterial infection that causes diarrhea. *C. diff* is not related to measles or influenza.

2. **Lyme disease** is the most frequently transmitted tick-borne disease. Chagas disease is caused by a parasite that is common in South and Central America.

3. The **Epstein-Barr virus** causes infectious mononucleosis. Human papillomavirus (HPV) is the most common sexually transmitted infection.

4. *Staphylococcus aureus* is the most common pathogen for pneumonia. *Escherichia coli* (bacteria) can cause diarrhea and often is associated with urinary tract infections. Although it can be associated with pneumonia, it is not the most common pathogen.

5. **Kaposi sarcoma** is most commonly associated with AIDS. The sarcoma is an opportunistic infection, meaning that it takes advantage of debilitated patients. Merkel cell carcinoma is primarily a skin cancer and not commonly associated with AIDS.

Coding

1. Western equine encephalitis
   A83.1 Western equine encephalitis
   Index: Encephalitis, Western equine

2. Cytomegaloviral mononucleosis
   B27.10 Cytomegaloviral mononucleosis without complications
   Index: Mononucleosis, infection, cytomegaloviral

3. Chickenpox
   B01.9 Varicella without complication
   Index: Chickenpox, *see Varicella*

4. Meningitis due to Lyme disease
   A69.21 Meningitis due to Lyme disease
   Index: Meningitis, in (due to) Lyme disease

5. Gonococcal conjunctivitis of the left eye
   A54.31 Gonococcal conjunctivitis
   Index: Conjunctivitis, in (due to) gonococci

6. Acute viral hepatitis C
   B17.10 Acute hepatitis C without hepatic coma
   Index: Hepatitis, viral, acute (this entry leads to unspecified code). Coders may review series of codes in this section to locate more specified code.
   Index: Hepatitis, C (viral), acute leads to B17.10

7. Shingles of the eyelids
   B02.39 Other herpes zoster eye disease
   Index: Shingles—*see Herpes, zoster*
   Herpes, zoster, eye (lid)

8. Toxic shock syndrome (*staphylococcus* identified as organism)
   A48.3 Toxic shock syndrome
   B95.8 Unspecified *staphylococcus* as the cause of disease classified elsewhere
   Index: Syndrome, toxic shock
   See note that states "use additional code to identify organism (B95, B96)."

9. Severe gastroenteritis due to *Salmonella* food poisoning
   A02.0 Salmonella enteritis
   Index: Poisoning, food, due to *salmonella* with gastroenteritis

10. Vulvovaginitis due to chlamydial infection
    A56.02 Chlamydial vulvovaginitis
    Index: Chlamydia, vulvovaginitis

Answers for Chapter 2: Neoplasms

Check Your Knowledge of Neoplasms

__B__ **1.** Adenoma of prostate

__M__ **2.** Infiltrating duct carcinoma of the breast

__B__ **3.** Osteofibroma of the femur (refers coder to bone)

__U__ **4.** Endometrioid adenoma (pathology report states borderline malignancy)

__M__ **5.** Hepatic mesenchymal sarcoma (refers coder to connective tissue)

Check Your Clinical Knowledge

1. The pathology report states that the patient has carcinoma in situ of the cervix. This morphology indicates that the cancer cells have **not invaded the surrounding tissues.**

2. **Melanoma** is most often identified as skin cancer.

3. A uterine leiomyoma is commonly known as a **fibroid.**

4. Condylomas are commonly known as **genital warts.**

5. An adenomatous polyp in the colon would be identified as a **benign** tumor.

Coding

1. Myxofibrosarcoma of the neck
   C49.0 Malignant neoplasm of connective and soft tissue of head, face, and neck
   Index: Myxofibrosarcoma—*see Neoplasm, connective tissue, malignant*

2. Female patient was diagnosed with carcinoma of the lower-inner quadrant of the right breast
   C50.311 Malignant neoplasm of lower-inner quadrant of right female breast
   Index: *see also Neoplasm by site, malignant*
   Neoplasm Table: primary site listed as C50.31- (must refer to Tabular List for sixth character, which identifies the laterality [right breast])

3. Malignant melanoma of the skin of the cheek
   C43.39 Malignant melanoma of other parts of the face
   Index: Melanoma, skin, cheek

4. Carcinoma of the upper lobe of the right lung with metastasis to the bone (spinal column)
   C34.11 Malignant neoplasm of upper lobe, right bronchus or lung
   C79.51 Secondary malignant neoplasm of bone
   Index: *see also Neoplasm by site, malignant*
   Code for lung from malignant primary column in Neoplasm table. Code for bone from malignant secondary column.

5. Adenocarcinoma of the prostate
   C61 Malignant neoplasm of prostate
   Index: Adenocarcinoma—*see also Neoplasm, malignant*
   Refer to Neoplasm table for site from Malignant Primary column.

6. Osteofibroma of the right femur
D16.21 Benign neoplasm of long bones of right lower limb
Index: Osteofibroma—see *Neoplasm bone, benign*

7. Condyloma acuminatum of the penis
A63.0 Anogenital (venereal) warts
Index: Condyloma, acuminatum
Note that this code is located in the Infectious and Parasitic Diseases chapter.

8. Diffuse lymphoblastic lymphoma (of lymph nodes of left axilla and arm)
C83.54 Lymphoblastic (diffuse) lymphoma, lymph nodes of axilla and upper limb
Index: Lymphoblastic—see *condition*
Lymphoma, lymphoblastic C83.5-

9. Mixed glioma of the right optic nerve
C72.31 Malignant neoplasm of right optic nerve
Index: Glioma, mixed, specific site—see *Neoplasm, malignant*
Neoplasm table: Nerve, optic (from Malignant primary column) C72.3-

10. Malignant melanoma of forehead
C43.39 Malignant melanoma, other parts of the face
Index: Melanoma, skin, forehead

Answers for Chapter 3: Diseases of the Blood and Blood-Forming Organs
Check Your Clinical Knowledge

Clinical Description	Diagnosis
1. __C__ 34-year-old man experiences excessive bleeding after surgery, reports that he bruised easily.	**A.** sickle cell disease
2. __A__ 5-year-old African American child reports abdominal pain and trouble breathing. Clinician notes delayed growth.	**B.** vitamin B deficiency

3. __B__ 22-year-old woman, who is a vegetarian, reports chronic fatigue, generalized aching, and insomnia.
C. von Willebrand disease

4. __E__ 5-year-old child is pale, tired, and irritable. Recently treated for digestive disorder. Reddish tint to urine.
D. Christmas disease (hemophilia B)

5. __D__ Child experiences excessive bleeding following circumcision. Lab results reveal hereditary clotting disorder.
E. hemolytic uremic syndrome

Coding

1. Posttraumatic cyst of the spleen
D73.4 Cyst of spleen
Index: Cyst, spleen NEC D73.4

2. Christmas disease (hemophilia B)
D67 Hereditary factor IX deficiency
Index: Christmas disease

3. Normocytic chronic blood loss anemia
D50.0 Iron deficiency anemia secondary to blood loss (chronic)
Index: Anemia, normocytic, due to blood loss (chronic)

4. Vitamin B12 deficiency anemia—vegan anemia
D51.3 Other dietary vitamin B12 deficiency anemia
Index: Anemia, vegan

5. Coagulation disorder, factor X
D68.2 Hereditary deficiency of other clotting factors
Index: Disorder, coagulation—see also *Defect, coagulation*
Defect, coagulation—see also *Deficiency, factor*
Deficiency, factor, X

Answers for Chapter 4: Endocrine, Nutritional, and Metabolic Diseases

Check Your Clinical Knowledge: Case Studies

Case Study # 1

This profile would best support which of the following diagnoses?

   a. Type 1 diabetes mellitus

   b. **Type 2 diabetes mellitus**

   c. Graves disease

   d. Hypothyroidism

Case Study # 2

This profile would best support which of the following diagnoses?

   a. Type 1 diabetes mellitus

   b. Type 2 diabetes mellitus

   c. **Graves disease**

   d. Hypothyroidism

Case Study # 3

This profile would best support which of the following diagnoses?

   a. **Type 1 diabetes mellitus**

   b. Type 2 diabetes mellitus

   c. Graves disease

   d. Hypothyroidism

Case Study # 4

This type of skin ulcer would be classified as:

   a. Decubitus

   b. Pressure ulcer

   c. **Nonpressure ulcer**

Coding

1. Graves disease

   E05.00 Thyrotoxicosis, with diffuse goiter, without thyrotoxic crisis or storm

   Index: Graves—see *Hyperthyroidism, with goiter*

2. Hyperkalemia

   E87.5 Hyperkalemia

   Index: Hyperkalemia

3. Vitamin B12 deficiency

   E53.8 Deficiency of other specified B group vitamins

   Index: Deficiency, vitamin B12

4. Diabetic cataract, Type 1 diabetic patient

   E10.36 Type 1 diabetes mellitus with diabetic cataract

   Index: diabetes, Type 1, with cataract

5. Type 1 diabetes with diabetic chronic skin ulcer of the left heel and midfoot *(breakdown of skin only)*

   E10.622 Type 1 diabetes mellitus with other skin ulcer *(see note that states to use additional code to identify the site of the ulcer [L code section])*

   L97.421 Nonpressure chronic ulcer of left heel and midfoot limited to breakdown of skin *(see note under L97 that instructs the coder to code first any associated underlying condition)*

   Index: diabetes, Type 1, with skin ulcer

   Ulcer, heel (see lower limb), heel, left, with skin breakdown only

Answers for Chapter 5: Mental, Behavioral, and Neurodevelopmental Disorders

Check Your Clinical Knowledge

Clinical Description	Diagnosis
1. __D__ inattentive, impulsive, and hyperactive	A. panic disorder
2. __C__ loss of interest, no pleasure in life	B. schizophrenia

3. __A__ episodes of palpitations, diaphoresis, fear of losing control

C. depression

4. __E__ flashbacks, nightmares, intrusive memories

D. attention-deficit disorder

5. __B__ delusional, hallucinations, disorganized thinking

E. posttraumatic stress syndrome

Coding

1. Anorexia nervosa—patient alternates between binge eating and purging

    F50.02 Anorexia nervosa, binge eating/pursing type

    Index: Anorexia, binge eating, with purging

2. Posttraumatic stress disorder, acute

    F43.11 Posttraumatic stress disorder, acute

    Index: Disorder, posttraumatic stress

3. Complete auditory hallucinations

    R44.0 Auditory hallucinations

    Index: hallucinations, auditory

    Note: This condition is classified in the chapter on Symptoms, Signs, and Abnormal Clinical and Laboratory Findings.

4. Bipolar disorder (current episode of depression), mild

    F31.31 Bipolar disorder, current episode depressed, mild

    Index: Disorder, biopolar, current episode, depressed without psychotic features, mild

5. Schizotypal personality disorder

    F21 Schizotypal disorder

    Index: Disorder, personality, schizotypal

Answers for Chapter 6: Diseases of Nervous System (Eyes and Ears)

Check Your Clinical Knowledge

1. The physician documents that the patient's middle ear infection was producing pus. Producing pus would be classified as **purulent.**

2. The elderly patient's eyelids were drooping and causing problems with vision. The physician scheduled the patient for surgery with the diagnosis of **dermatochalasis.**

3. The physician noted that the patient's **intractable** pain was severe, constant, and not curable.

4. The documentation states that the patient's eye (iris and ciliary body) is swollen and inflamed. The physician concludes with the diagnosis of **iridocyclitis.**

5. The pathology report describes the **pterygium** as a noncancerous growth of the conjunctiva.

Coding

1. Left ulnar nerve entrapment at the elbow

    G56.22 Lesion of ulnar nerve, left side

    Index: Entrapment, nerve—*see Neuropathy entrapment*

    Index: Neuropathy, entrapment, ulnar nerve G56.2-

2. Left tympanic membrane perforation

    H72.92 Unspecified perforation of tympanic membrane, left ear

    Index: Perforation, tympanic H72.9-

3. Intracranial meningioma

    D32.0 Benign neoplasm of cerebral meninges

    Index: Meningioma—*see Neoplasm, meninges, benign*

4. Retinal detachment, left eye

   H33.22 Serous retinal detachment, left eye

   Index: Detachment, retina H33.2-

5. Carpal tunnel compression, left, severe

   G56.02 Carpal tunnel syndrome, left side

   Index: Compression, nerve, median (in carpal tunnel)—see *Syndrome, carpal tunnel*

   Index: Syndrome, carpal tunnel G56.0-

   Note: On this case, knowledge of anatomy is important. Reference a website for clarification of the disease process associated with carpal tunnel syndrome.

6. Patient seen in emergency department as a result of an injury at work. Diagnosis: Foreign body of left eye—sliver of metal located in cornea

   T15.02XA Foreign body, in cornea, left eye (seventh character for "initial encounter")

   Index: Foreign body, cornea T15.0 or reference Foreign body, eye cornea— see *Foreign body cornea T15.0-*

   Note: This is not in the Eye chapter but classified in the Injury category.

7. Dermatochalasis of bilateral upper eyelids

   H02.834 Dermatochalasis of left upper eyelid

   H02.831 Dermatochalasis of right upper eyelid

   Index: Dermatochalasis, left and right, upper

8. Acute otitis media, left, producing pus

   H66.002 Acute suppurative otitis media without spontaneous rupture of ear drum, left ear

   Index: Otitis, media, acute, purulent—see *Otitis, media, suppurative, acute.* Note that purulent *means "pus producing."*

9. Classic migraine, intractable with aura

   G43.119 Migraine with aura, intractable, without status migrainosus

   Index: Migraine, with aura, intractable, without status migrainosus

10. Spastic hemiplegia of right (dominant) side

G81.11 Spastic hemiplegia affecting right dominant side

Index: Hemiplegia, spastic G81.1-

Note under G81 specifies that this category is used only when there is not further specificity. If the hemiplegia follows a stroke, coders are referred to the I69 code section.

Answers for Chapter 7: Diseases of the Circulatory System

Check Your Knowledge of Anatomy

Refer to Figure A-1

1. Aortic valve

2. Mitral valve

3. Pulmonic valve

4. Tricuspid valve

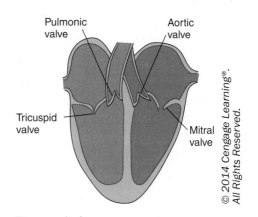

Figure A-1

Check Your Clinical Knowledge

1. The patient's blood pressure is 150/85. The number 85 is referred to as the **diastolic** pressure.

2. A(n) **thrombus** is a blood clot that forms in the vessel and *does not* move to another area of the body.

3. As a result of a stroke, the patient has difficulty swallowing and is ordered therapy for the treatment of **dysphagia.**

4. The documentation in the health records indicates that the patient has

a rapid heart rate, which supports the diagnosis of **tachycardia.**

5. The surgeon documented that the **carotid** artery in the neck was occluded and caused the stroke.

Coding

1. Acute, diastolic congestive heart failure

   I50.31 Acute diastolic (congestive) heart failure

   Index: Failure, heart, diastolic, acute

2. Rheumatic aortic valve stenosis

   I06.0 Rheumatic aortic stenosis

   Index: Stenosis, aortic, rheumatic

3. Pulmonary embolism with acute cor pulmonale

   I26.09 Other pulmonary embolism with acute cor pulmonale

   Index: Embolism, pulmonary, with acute cor poulmonale

4. Acute posterolateral-transmural myocardial infarction (ST elevation)

   I21.29 ST Elevation myocardial infarction (STEMI) involving other sites

   Index: Infarction, myocardial, ST elevation, posterior

5. Hypertensive heart disease with chronic (systolic and diastolic) heart failure

   I11.0 Hypertensive heart disease with heart failure

   I50.42 Chronic combined systolic (congestive) and diastolic (congestive) heart failure

   Index: Disease, heart, hypertensive—see Hypertension, heart

   Index: Hypertensive, heart with heart failure

   See note under code I11.0 to use additional code to identify type of heart failure.

6. Cerebrovascular accident due to thrombosis of left vertebral artery

   I63.012 Cerebral infarction due to thrombosis of left vertebral artery

   Index: Accident, cerebrovascular leads to a generic I63.9 code

   Index: Thrombosis, artery, vertebral—see Occlusion, artery, vertebral

Index: Occlusion, artery, vertebral with infarction, due to thrombosis I63.01-

In this case, the index sends the coder to several different entries. It might have been best to review the selection in the I63 section and carefully read the choices for an accurate code assignment.

7. Premature ventricular contractions

   I49.3 Ventricular premature depolarization

   Index: Contractions, premature, ventricular

8. Cerebrovascular infarction due to embolism of right middle cerebral artery

   I63.411 Cerebral infarction due to embolism of right middle cerebral artery

   Index: Infarct, Infarction, cerebral, due to embolism, cerebral arteries I63.4-

9. Left bundle branch block

   I44.7 Left bundle branch block, unspecified

   Index: Block, bundle-branch, left

10. Patient treated in the outpatient clinic for dysphagia (pharyngeal phase) as a residual from a previous intracerebral hemorrhage

    I69.191 Dysphagia following nontraumatic intracerebral hemorrhage

    R13.13 Dysphagia pharyngeal phase

    Index: Dysphagia, following, intracerebral hemorrhage

    Note: See the note to guide the coder to use an additional code to identify the type of dysphagia.

Answers for Chapter 8: Diseases of the Respiratory System

Check Your Knowledge of Anatomy

Refer to Figure A-2

1. Pharynx
2. Larynx
3. Trachea
4. Alveoli
5. Bronchiole

6. Bronchus
7. Right Lung
8. Mouth
9. Nasal cavity

Check Your Clinical Knowledge

1. The patient has a piece of candy stuck in his throat that is causing irritation. The physician documents examination of the **pharynx.**

2. The physician documents that the patient has a buildup of fluid in the air sacs of the lungs. This documentation supports the diagnosis of **pulmonary edema.**

3. The physician documents that the patient has wheezing, shortness of breath, and chest tightness. It was noted that the family recently adopted a cat. The documentation supports the diagnosis of **asthma.**

4. The physician notes that there is swelling and mucus buildup in the smallest air passages in the lungs, or the **bronchioles.**

5. The physician documents that the patient has a bacterial pneumonia. The laboratory test revealed *Pseudomonas.*

Coding

1. Hypertrophic adenoids and tonsils
   J35.3 Hypertrophy of tonsils with hypertrophy of adenoids
   Index: Hypertrophy, tonsils with adenoids

2. Chronic pulmonary edema
   J81.1 Chronic pulmonary edema
   Index: Edema, pulmonary—see *Edema, lung*
   Index: Edema, lung, chronic

3. Obstructive rhinitis
   J31.0 Chronic rhinitis
   Index: Rhinitis (obstructive)

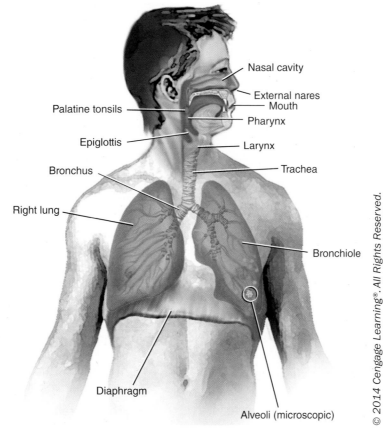

Nasal cavity
External nares
Mouth
Palatine tonsils
Pharynx
Epiglottis
Larynx
Bronchus
Trachea
Right lung
Bronchiole
Diaphragm
Alveoli (microscopic)

Figure A-2

4. Chronic obstructive pulmonary disease (COPD) with acute bronchitis

   J44.0 Chronic obstructive pulmonary disease with acute lower respiratory infection

   Index: Disease, pulmonary, chronic obstructive, with acute bronchitis

5. Bilateral, complete cleft palate with cleft lip

   Q37.8 Unspecified cleft palate with bilateral cleft lip

   Index: Cleft, lip, bilateral with cleft palate Q37.9

   Note: This condition is classified in the Congenital chapter.

6. Maxillary nasal polyp

   J33.8 Other polyp of sinus

   Index: Polyp, maxillary

7. Severe, persistent asthma with acute exacerbation

   J45.51 Severe persistent with (acute) exacerbation

   Index: Asthma, persistent, severe with exacerbation (acute)

8. Bronchopneumonia due to *staphylococci*

   J15.20 Pneumonia due to *staphylococcus*, unspecified

   Index: Pneumonia, broncho, staphylococcal—*see Pneumonia, staphylococcal*

   Index: Pneumonia, staphylococcal

9. Acute pharyngitis due to the flu

   J10.1 Influenza due to other identified influenza virus with other respiratory manifestations

   Index: Pharyngitis with influenza, flu, or grippe—*see Influenza, with respiratory manifestations*

   Index: Influenza, with respiratory manifestations

10. A 6-year-old child is seen for acute respiratory distress syndrome

    J80 Acute respiratory distress syndrome

    Index: Syndrome, respiratory, distress, acute, child

Note: Although the Alphabetic Index provides separate entries for child and adult, the code is the same.

Answers for Chapter 9: Diseases of the Digestive System

Check Your Knowledge of Anatomy

Refer to Figure A-3

1. Oral cavity
2. Pharynx
3. Esophagus
4. Ascending colon
5. Descending colon
6. Appendix
7. Anus
8. Rectum
9. Sigmoid colon
10. Ileum
11. Jejunum
12. Duodenum

Check Your Clinical Knowledge

1. The surgeon noted that stones were located in the bile duct and documented the diagnosis of **choledocholithiasis.**

2. The operative report explained that an excessive amount of fluid was located in the peritoneal cavity. This statement was consistent with the postoperative diagnosis of **ascites.**

3. The pathology report revealed that the gallbladder was inflamed, which supported the postoperative diagnosis of **cholecystitis.**

4. The physical examination revealed a protrusion of the intestine through a weakening of the abdominal wall near the groin. This finding supports the diagnosis of a **femoral** hernia.

5. The operative report revealed a stricture in the small intestine, supporting documentation of a narrowing of the **ileum.**

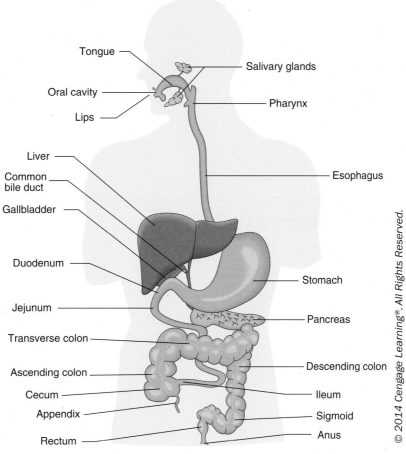

Tongue

Salivary glands

Oral cavity

Lips

Pharynx

Liver

Esophagus

Common bile duct

Gallbladder

Duodenum

Stomach

Jejunum

Pancreas

Transverse colon

Ascending colon

Descending colon

Cecum

Ileum

Appendix

Sigmoid

Rectum

Anus

Figure A-3

Coding

1. Recurrent distal esophageal stricture
   K22.2 Esophageal obstruction
   Index: Stricture, esophagus

2. Chronic hepatic failure
   K72.10 Chronic hepatic failure without coma
   Index: Failure, hepatic, chronic

3. Gastrointestinal bleeding (GI) due to angiodysplasia of stomach and duodenum
   K31.811 Angiodysplasia of stomach and duodenum with bleeding
   Index: Angiodysplasia, stomach, with bleeding

4. Alcoholic hepatitis with ascites
   K70.11 Alcoholic hepatitis with ascites
   Index: Hepatitis, alcoholic with ascites

5. Perforated acute duodenal ulcer
   K26.1 Acute duodenal ulcer with perforation
   Index: Ulcer, duodenum, acute, with perforation

6. Preoperative diagnosis: Polyp of the colon.
   Pathology report states adenocarcinoma of the ascending colon
   C18.2 Malignant neoplasm of ascending colon
   Index: Adenocarcinoma—*see Neoplasm, malignant*
   Index: Neoplasm table: Colon—*see Neoplasm, intestine, large*
   Neoplasm, intestine, large, colon, ascending

7. Diverticulosis of ileum with hemorrhaging
   K57.11 Diverticulosis of small intestine without perforation or abscess with bleeding
   Index: Diverticulosis, small intestine with bleeding

8. External hemorrhoids
   K64.4 Residual hemorrhoidal skin tags
   Index: Hemorrhoids, external

9. Acute gastritis with hemorrhaging

K29.01 Acute gastritis with bleeding

Index: Gastritis, acute, with bleeding

10. Ulcerated esophageal varices

I85.00 Esophageal varices without bleeding

Index: Varices—*see Varix*

Index: Varix, esophagus

Note: This code is located in the Circulatory chapter.

Answers for Chapter 10: Diseases of the Skin and Subcutaneous Tissue

Check Your Knowledge of Anatomy

Refer to Figure A-4

1. Sweat pore
2. Epidermis
3. Dermis
4. Subcutaneous fatty tissue
5. Sweat gland
6. Papilla of hair
7. Hair follicle
8. Sebaceous (oil) gland
9. Arrector pili muscle
10. Hair shaft

Check Your Clinical Knowledge

1. **Impetigo** is an extremely contagious skin disease that most commonly affects the face and hands and is caused by streptococcal and staphylococcal bacteria. Plantar warts are a chronic skin condition with a cauliflower-like appearance that are present on the sole of the foot.

2. **Psoriasis,** a noncontagious chronic skin disease, is characterized by a rapid replacement of epidermal cells that appears as red raised lesions with silvery colored scales. Candidiasis is commonly known as thrush and is caused by a fungal infection.

3. Skin redness, also known as **erythema,** is a common sign that occurs for many conditions of the integumentary system. Hematoma is a collection of blood in the tissues of the skin or in an organ, commonly known as a bruise or contusion.

4. Erosion of the skin or mucous membrane that results in tissue loss due to prolonged pressure on the affected area is known as a pressure ulcer or a **decubitus** ulcer. A papule is a small raised lesion.

5. A boil, also known as a **furuncle,** is a small abscess that occurs in the tissues of the skin generally around a hair follicle. A carbuncle is an abscess that involves several furuncles and arises in a cluster of hair follicles.

Coding

1. Acute lymphadenitis of axilla

L04.2 Acute lymphadenitis of upper limb

Index: Lymphadenitis, acute, axilla

2. Circumscribed neurodermatitis

L28.0 Lichen simplex chronicus

Index: Neurodermatitis

3. Yellow nail syndrome

L60.5 Yellow nail syndrome

Index: Syndrome, yellow nail

4. Urticaria due to cold

L50.2 Urticaria due to cold and heat

Index: Urticaria, due to cold and heat

5. Acute lymphangitis of left arm

L03.124 Acute lymphangitis of left upper limb

Index: Lymphangitis, acute, arm—*see Lymphangitis, acute, upper limb*

6. Dry skin dermatitis

L85.3 Xerosis cutis

Index: Dermatitis, dry skin

7. Pressure sore of elbow, stage I

L89.001 Pressure ulcer of unspecified elbow, stage I

Index: sore, pressure—*see Ulcer, pressure, by site*

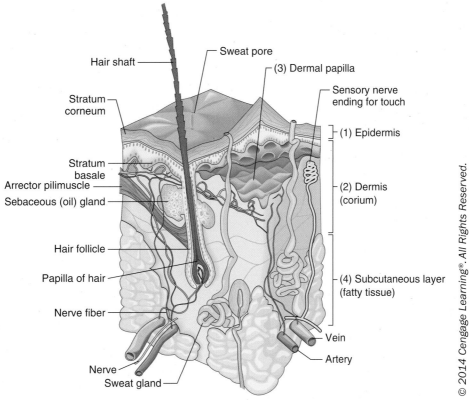

Hair shaft

Sweat pore

(3) Dermal papilla

Sensory nerve ending for touch

Stratum corneum

(1) Epidermis

Stratum basale

(2) Dermis (corium)

Arrector pilimuscle

Sebaceous (oil) gland

Hair follicle

Papilla of hair

(4) Subcutaneous layer (fatty tissue)

Nerve fiber

Vein

Artery

Nerve

Sweat gland

Figure A-4

8. Pilonidal cyst with abscess

L05.01 Pilonidal cyst with abscess

Index: Cyst, pilonidal, with abscess

9. Allergic dermatitis due to contact with chromium, accidental, initial visit

T56.2x1A Toxic effect of chromium and its compounds, accidental (unintentional), initial visit

L23.0 Allergic contact dermatitis due to metals

Index: Dermatitis, contact, allergic, due to chromium

In the Tabular List an instructional notation appears to "Code first (T36-T65) to identify drug or substance." Reference the Drugs and Chemical table under the term "Chromium." Select the code from the column entitled Poisoning, Accidental (unintentional).

Under category T56 there is a note to add an appropriate seventh character.

10. Androgenic alopecia

L64.9 Androgenic alopecia, unspecified

Index: Alopecia, androgenic

Answers for Chapter 11: Diseases of the Musculoskeletal System and Connective Tissue

Check Your Understanding of Anatomy and Disorders

A. Refer to Figure A-5a

1. Scoliosis

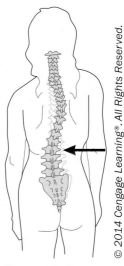

Figure A-5a

A. Refer to Figure A-5b

   2. Kyphosis

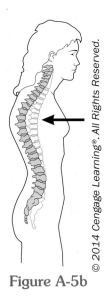

Figure A-5b

A. Refer to Figure A-5c

   3. Lordosis

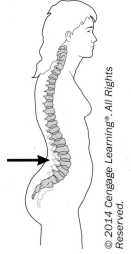

Figure A-5c

B. Refer to Figure A-6

   1. Vertebral body

   2. Intervertebral disc

   3. Cervical vertebrae

   4. Thoracic (dorsal) vertebrae

   5. Lumbar vertebrae

   6. Sacrum

   7. Coccyx

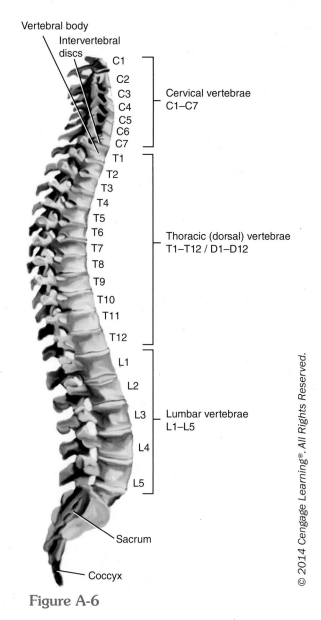

Vertebral body
Intervertebral discs
C1
C2
C3
C4
C5
C6
C7
Cervical vertebrae C1–C7
T1
T2
T3
T4
T5
T6
T7
T8
T9
T10
T11
T12
Thoracic (dorsal) vertebrae T1–T12 / D1–D12
L1
L2
L3
L4
L5
Lumbar vertebrae L1–L5
Sacrum
Coccyx

Figure A-6

Check Your Clinical Knowledge

1. **Osteoporosis** is a metabolic disease that causes the bone to have a Swiss cheese–like appearance that leads to bone mass loss. Arthritis means an inflammation of a joint.

2. The term "bunion" is commonly used for **hallux valgus,** a deformity that affects the metatarsophalangeal joint of the big toe. Rheumatoid arthritis is an autoimmune disorder that affects the joints and connective tissue of the entire body.

3. The physician documents the following: "In the patient's right hand there is fusion and total loss of joint function." This would suggest that the patient has **ankylosis** of the hand. Bursitis is the inflammation of a bursa which is the fluid-filled sac near a joint.

4. **Osteomalacia** is caused by a deficiency of vitamin D and results in the softening of the bones. Osteomyelitis is an inflammation of the bone that is most commonly caused by the pathogen *Staphylococcus aureus*.

5. An **electromyography** is used to evaluate muscle disorders by inserting a small needle into the muscle tissue and recording the electrical activity. A dual-energy X-ray absorptiometry scan is used to confirm low bone mass.

Coding

1. Juvenile osteochondrosis of pelvis
   M91.0 Juvenile osteochondrosis of pelvis
   Index: Osteochondrosis, juvenile, hip and pelvis, pelvis

2. Rheumatoid vasculitis with rheumatoid arthritis of left shoulder
   M05.212 Rheumatoid vasculitis with rheumatoid arthritis of left shoulder
   Index: Vasculitis, rheumatoid—*see Rheumatoid, vasculitis. Then reference Rheumatoid, vasculitis, shoulder*

3. Rheumatoid bursitis of the right foot and ankle
   M06.271 Rheumatoid bursitis of the right foot and ankle
   Index: Bursitis, rheumatoid, ankle, foot joint

4. Acute gout flare
   M10.9 Gout, unspecified
   Index: Gout, (acute)

5. Left foot, acquired hallux rigidus
   M20.22 Hallux rigidus, left foot
   Index: Hallux, rigidus (acquired)

6. Acquired clubfoot of right foot
   M21.541 Acquired clubfoot, right foot
   Index: Clubfoot, acquired—*see Deformity, limb, clubfoot*

7. Recurrent subluxation of patella, left knee
   M22.12 Recurrent subluxation of patella, left knee
   Index: Subluxation, patella, recurrent (nontraumatic)—*see Dislocation, patella, recurrent, incomplete*

8. Loose body in third left toe joint
   M24.075 Loose body in left toe joint(s)
   Index: Loose, body, joint, toe

9. Myositis ossificans progressiva, left upper arm
   M61.122 Myositis ossificans progressiva, left upper arm
   Index: Myositis, ossificans, progressive, upper arm

10. Right hip abscess of bursa caused by *Staphylococcus aureus*
    M71.051 Abscess of bursa, right hip
    B95.61 *Staphylococcus aureus* as the cause of diseases classified elsewhere
    Index: Abscess, bursa, hip. *Note in Tabular List under M71.0 instructs coder to "Use additional code (B95.-, B96.-) to identify causative organism."*

Answers for Chapter 12: Diseases of the Genitourinary System

Check Your Understanding of Anatomy and Disorders

A. Refer to Figure A-7

1. Left renal artery
2. Adrenal suprarenal glands
3. Left kidney
4. Urinary bladder
5. Prostate gland
6. Urethra
7. Urethral meatus
8. Ureteral orifices
9. Right and left ureters

10. Renal medulla
11. Renal cortex
12. Right kidney

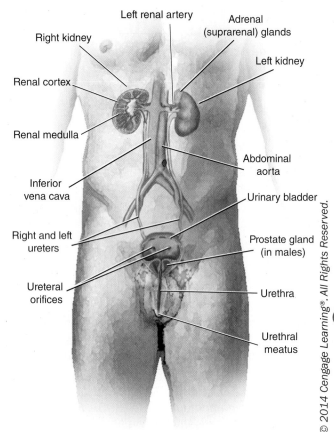

Figure A-7

B. Refer to Figure A-8

1. Ureter
2. Ovary
3. Cervix of uterus
4. Anus
5. Fallopian tube
6. Body of uterus
7. Urinary bladder
8. Clitoris
9. Urethra
10. Vagina

Check Your Clinical Knowledge

1. An inflammation of the fallopian tube is known as **salpingitis.** Oophoritis is an inflammation of the ovaries.

2. Patients with end-stage renal disease require **dialysis.** Insulin is required for patients with some forms of diabetes.

3. A test used to determine the levels of urea nitrogen or waste products in the blood is a **BUN** test. A urine C&S shows the number of white cells or bacteria in the urine, type of bacteria present, and effective antibiotic to prescribe for treatment.

4. **Polycystic disease,** an inherited disease, causes enlargement of both kidneys due to the formation of multiple grape-like cysts. Renal failure occurs when the kidneys fail to cleanse the blood of waste products.

5. **Stress** incontinence occurs when a person is unable to hold urine when he or she coughs, sneezes, or laughs. Overflow incontinence occurs when the bladder is not properly emptying and leaks when overfilled.

Coding

1. Calculus in urethra
   N21.1 Calculus in urethra
   Index: Calculus, urethra

2. Urinary tract obstruction
   N13.9 Obstructive and reflux uropathy, unspecified
   Index: Obstruction, urinary, organ or tract

3. Prostatic stone
   N42.0 Calculus of prostate
   Index: Stone(s) (see also Calculus), prostate

4. Irregular periods
   N92.6 Irregular menstruation, unspecified
   Index: Periods—see also Menstruation. Menstruation, irregular

5. Paravaginal cystocele
   N81.12 Cystocele, lateral
   Index: Cystocele, female, paravaginal

6. Segmental fat necrosis of breast
   N64.1 Fat necrosis of breast
   Index: Necrosis, fat, breast

7. Benign cyst of prepuce
   N47.4 Benign cyst of prepuce
   Index: Cyst, prepuce

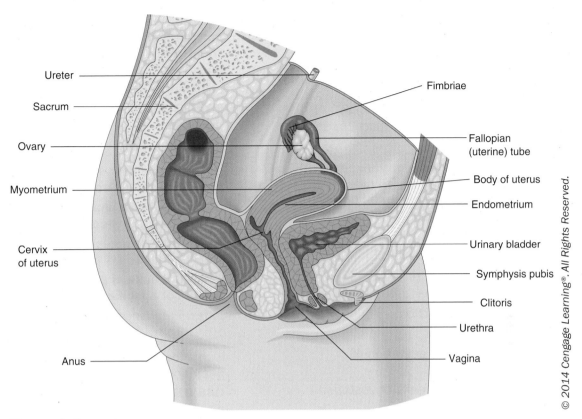

Figure A-8

8. Acquired bladder-neck stenosis
   N32.0 Bladder neck obstruction
   Index: Stenosis, bladder-neck (acquired)

9. Destrusor muscle hyperactivity
   N32.81 Overactive bladder
   Index: Hyperactive, hyperactivity, destrusor muscle

10. Acute nephritis
    N00.9 Acute nephritic syndrome with unspecified morphologic changes
    Index: Nephritis, acute

Answers for Chapter 13: Pregnancy, Childbirth, and the Puerperium

Check Your ICD-10-CM Knowledge

1. ICD-10-CM defines the **second** trimester from 14 weeks 0 days to less than 28 weeks 0 days. ICD-10-CM defines the third trimester from 28 weeks 0 days until delivery.

2. A seventh character of 0 for code O33.5xx0 denotes **single gestation.** A seventh character of 1 for code O33.5xx1 denotes fetus 1.

3. Obstetric **hematoma of vulva** is reported with code O71.7. Obstetric damage to coccyx is reported with code O71.6.

4. **Rupture of fallopian tube due to pregnancy** is classified to code O00.1. Mural pregnancy is classified to code O00.8.

5. A young primigravida, as defined by ICD-10-CM, is a woman who is less than **16** years old at expected date of delivery.

Check Your Clinical Knowledge

1. The most common location of an ectopic pregnancy is the **fallopian tubes.** The cervix is not a common site for an ectopic pregnancy.

2. Excessive vomiting during pregnancy is known as **hyperemesis gravidarum.** A miscarriage is a spontaneous abortion.

3. **Placenta previa** is the abnormal positioning of the placenta in the lower uterus. Abruptio placentae is the sudden separation of the placenta from the uterine wall prior to or at the time of labor.

4. The letters in HELLP syndrome refer to **hemolysis**, elevated liver function, and low platelet level.

5. Pre-eclampsia is a serious condition of pregnancy characterized by hypertension, **edema,** and proteinuria. Coma occurs in eclampsia.

Coding

1. Missed abortion at 17 weeks' gestation with retention of dead fetus

   O02.1 Missed abortion

   Index: Abortion, missed

   Z3A.17 17 weeks gestation of pregnancy

   Index: Pregnancy, weeks of gestation

2. 24-week OB visit for 14-year-old primigravida patient

   O09.612 Supervision of young primigravida, second trimester

   Index: Pregnancy, supervision, very young mother, primigravida

   Z3A.24 24 weeks gestation of pregnancy

   Index: Pregnancy, weeks of gestation

3. Tubal abortion

   O00.1 Tubal pregnancy

   Index: Abortion, tubal

   Z3A.00 Weeks of gestation of pregnancy not specified

   Index: Pregnancy, weeks of gestation

4. Eclampsia during 29th week of pregnancy

   O15.03 Eclampsia in pregnancy, third trimester

   Index: Eclampsia, pregnancy

   Z3A.29 29 weeks gestation of pregnancy

   Index: Pregnancy, weeks of gestation

5. Antepartum hemorrhage with coagulation defect at 30 weeks' gestation

   O46.003 Antepartum hemorrhage with coagulation defect, unspecified, third trimester

   Index: Hemorrhage, antepartum, with coagulation defect

   Z3A.30 30 weeks gestation of pregnancy

   Index: Pregnancy, weeks of gestation

6. Diabetes mellitus arising during pregnancy controlled by diet

   O24.410 Gestational diabetes mellitus in pregnancy, diet-controlled

   Index: Diabetes, gestational, diet-controlled

   Z3A.00 Weeks of gestation of pregnancy not specified

   Index: Pregnancy, weeks of gestation

7. Premature separation of placenta with afibrinogenemia, at 31 weeks' gestation

   O45.013 Premature separation of placenta with afibrinogenemia, third trimester

   Index: Pregnancy, complicated by, premature separation of placenta O45—see also Abruptio placentae. Reference Abruptio placentae, with afibrinogenemia

   Z3A.31 31 weeks gestation of pregnancy

   Index: Pregnancy, weeks of gestation

8. *Streptococcus* group A infection of bladder following delivery

   O86.22 Infection of bladder following delivery

   B95.0 *Streptococcus*, group A, as the cause of diseases classified elsewhere

   Index: Puerperal, infection, urinary, bladder

   The Tabular List for code O86.22 instructs the coder to "Use additional code (B95-B97) to identify infectious agent."

   Reference: Infection, as cause of disease classified elsewhere, B95.5.

   Code B95.5 classifies unspecified streptococcus; therefore, code B95.0 should be used to report group A.

9. Cracked nipple due to breast-feeding

O92.13 Cracked nipple associated with lactation

Index: Cracked nipple, associated with lactation

10. Cesarean delivery of 7-pound 11-ounce baby girl *(assign an Outcome of Delivery code)*

O82 Encounter for cesarean delivery without indication

Z37.0 Single liveborn

Index: Delivery, cesarean, without indication

Outcome of delivery, single, liveborn

Z3A.00 Weeks of gestation of pregnancy not specified

Index: Pregnancy, weeks of gestation

Answers for Chapter 14: Certain Conditions Originating in the Perinatal Period and Congenital Malformations, Deformations, and Chromosomal Abnormalities

Check Your Knowledge of Conditions

Congenital Conditions

✓ **1.** Pentalogy of Fallot

_____ **2.** Respiratory distress syndrome

_____ **3.** Sepsis of newborn due to *E. coli*

✓ **4.** Cleft palate with bilateral cleft lip

_____ **5.** Neonatal cerebral ischemia

✓ **6.** Transposition of colon

✓ **7.** Complex syndactyly of fingers with synostosis

_____ **8.** Traumatic glaucoma of newborn

_____ **9.** Neonatal melena

✓ **10.** Van der Woude's syndrome

Check Your Clinical Knowledge

1. **Spina bifida** is a congenital disorder in which the posterior portion of the vertebrae of the bony spinal column fails to close over the spinal cord. Cerebral palsy is a paralysis that results from inadequate blood or oxygen supply to the brain during fetal development, the birthing process, or in infancy.

2. **Tetralogy of Fallot** is a combination of four defects of the heart. (Tetralogy of Fallot, hemophilia) Hemophilia is a hereditary X-linked bleeding disorder.

3. **Hirschsprung's disease** typically impacts the sigmoid colon and is due to an absence of nerves therefore causing a lack of peristalsis. Hypospadias is a congenital condition in which there is an abnormal opening of the male urinary meatus on the undersurface of the penis.

4. Congenital varicella is a congenital **viral** disease.

5. **Anencephaly** occurs early in gestation and is a severe form of neural tube deficit with the failure of the cephalic aspect of the neural tube to close. Talipes equinovarus, commonly known as clubfoot, occurs when there is a deformity of the anterior half of the foot and the foot is adducted and inverted.

Coding

1. Lumbar spina bifida with hydrocephalus

Q05.2 Lumbar spina bifida with hydrocephalus

Index: Spina bifida, lumbar, with hydrocephalus

2. Rupture of the liver due to birth injury

P15.0 Birth injury to liver

Index: Birth, injury, liver

3. Newborn impacted by in utero exposure to tobacco smoke

P04.2 Newborn (suspected to be) affected by maternal use of tobacco

Index: Tobacco (nicotine), maternal use, affecting newborn

4. Newborn type II, respiratory distress syndrome

   P22.1 Transient tachypnea of newborn

   Index: Syndrome, respiratory, distress, newborn, type II

5. Cephalhematoma due to birth injury

   P12.0 Cephalhematoma due to birth injury

   Index: Cephalhematoma, newborn (birth injury)

6. Congenital funnel chest

   Q67.6 Pectus excavatum

   Index: Funnel, chest, congenital

7. Birth weight of newborn, 525 grams

   P07.02 Extremely low birth weight of newborn, 500–749 grams

   Index: Low, birth weight, extreme, with weight of, 500–749 grams

8. Acidosis of newborn

   P84 Other problems with newborn

   Index: Acidosis, newborn

9. Transient neonatal diabetes mellitus

   P70.2 Neonatal diabetes mellitus

   Index: Diabetes, neonatal (transient)

10. Neonatal rectal hemorrhage

    P54.2 Neonatal rectal hemorrhage

    Index: Hemorrhage, rectum, newborn

Answers for Chapter 15: Symptoms, Signs, and Abnormal Clinical and Laboratory Findings, Not Elsewhere Classified

Check Your Knowledge

1. Circulatory
2. Genitourinary
3. Skin and subcutaneous tissue
4. Respiratory
5. Digestive

Check Your Clinical Knowledge

Clinical Description		Diagnosis
1. __C__ elevated PSA		A. seizure activity
2. __E__ abnormal EKG		B. visual impairment
3. __A__ abnormal EEG		C. prostate cancer
4. __B__ abnormal ERG		D. diabetes mellitus
5. __D__ elevated fasting glucose		E. myocardial infarction

Coding

1. Elevated CRP

   R79.82 Elevated C-reactive protein (CRP)

   Index: Elevated, C-reactive protein (CRP)

2. Fluid retention

   R60.9 Edema, unspecified

   Index: Retention, fluid

3. Painful urination

   R30.9 Painful micturition, unspecified

   Index: Urination, painful

4. Spastic gait

   R26.1 Paralytic gait

   Index: Gait abnormality, spastic

5. Abnormal bowel sounds

   R19.15 Other abnormal bowel sounds

   Index: Abnormal, bowel sounds

6. Abnormal level of cocaine in the blood

   R78.2 Finding of cocaine in blood

   Index: Findings, abnormal, inconclusive, without diagnosis, in blood (of substance not normally found in blood), cocaine

7. Abnormal liver function study

R94.5 Abnormal results of liver function studies

Index: Findings, abnormal, inconclusive, without diagnosis, function study, liver

8. Elevated levels of steroids in urine

R82.5 Elevated urine levels of drugs, medicaments, and biological substances

Index: Elevated, elevation, urine level of, steroids

9. Decreased sexual desire

R68.82 Decreased libido

Index: Decrease(d), sexual desire

10. Patient is a 10-day-old infant with excessive crying

R68.11 Excessive crying of infant (baby)

Index: Excess, excessive, excessively, crying, in infant

Answers for Chapter 16: Injuries, Poisoning, and Certain Other Consequences of External Causes

Check Your Knowledge of Anatomy

Refer to Figure A-9

1. Skull
2. Maxilla
3. Mandible
4. Clavicle
5. Sternum
6. Humerus
7. Ribs
8. Vertebral column
9. Ilium
10. Radius
11. Pubis
12. Ulna
13. Carpals
14. Metacarpals
15. Phalanges of hand
16. Ischium
17. Femur
18. Patella
19. Tibia
20. Fibula
21. Tarsals
22. Metatarsals
23. Phalanges of foot

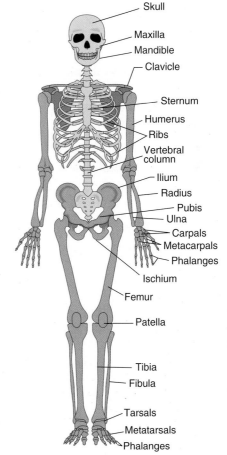

Appendicular skeleton (blue)
Axial skeleton (grey)

Figure A-9

Coding

1. Complete traumatic amputation of left ear

   S08.112A Complete traumatic amputation of left ear

   Index: Amputation, traumatic, ear (complete)

2. Subsequent encounter for puncture wound of the scalp

   S01.03xD Puncture wound without foreign body of scalp

   Index: Puncture, scalp

3. Right eye, penetrating wound of orbit

   S05.41xA Penetrating wound of orbit with or without foreign body, right eye

   Index: Wound, open, orbit—*see Wound, open, ocular, orbit*

4. Posterior displaced Type II dens fracture, subsequent encounter with routine healing

   S12.111D Posterior displaced Type II dens fracture

   Index: Fracture, neck, cervical vertebra, second, dens, posterior

5. Contusion of left front wall of thorax

   S20.212A Contusion of left front wall of thorax

   Index: Contusion, thorax, front

6. Rejection of bone marrow transplant

   T86.01 Bone marrow transplant rejection

   Index: Rejection, bone, marrow

7. Sexual abuse of child

   T74.22xA Child sexual abuse, confirmed

   Index: Abuse, sexual—*see Maltreatment, sexual abuse. Reference Maltreatment, child, sexual abuse, confirmed*

8. Local infection due to port-a-cath

   T80.212A Local infection due to central venous catheter, port or reservoir

   Index: Infection, due to, central venous catheter, port or reservoir

9. Open transverse fracture of the shaft of the right femur, displaced

   S72.321B Displaced transverse fracture of shaft of right femur

   Index: Fracture, femur, shaft, transverse

10. Sprain in left hip iliofemoral ligament, third follow-up visit

    S73.112D Iliofemoral ligament sprain of left hip

    Index: Sprain, hip, iliofemoral ligament

Answers for Chapter 17: External Causes of Morbidity

Check Your Knowledge of ICD-10-CM

1. aircraft
2. ten
3. nontraffic
4. three-wheeled
5. pedestrian

Coding

1. Tripping over carpet at patient's single family home in bedroom while rough housing *(in addition to an External Cause code, assign a code for both the Place of Occurrence [Y92-] and Activity [Y93-])*

   W22.8xxA Striking against or struck by other objects

   Index to External Cause: Tripping, over, carpet, rug or (small) object

   Y92.013 Bedroom of single family (private) house as the place of occurrence of the external cause

   Index to External Cause: Place of occurrence, residence, house, single family, bedroom

   Y93.83 Rough housing and horseplay

   Index to External Cause: Activity, rough housing and horseplay

2. Bitten by horse
   W55.11xA Bitten by horse
   Index to External Cause: Bite, horse

3. Fall into hole
   W17.2xxA Fall into hole
   Index to External Cause: Fall, falling, into, hole

4. Gored by goat
   W55.32xA Struck by other hoof stock
   Index to External Cause: Contact with goat, strike

5. Hypodermic needle stick
   W46.0xxA Contact with hypodermic needle
   Index to External Cause: Contract with, needle, hypodermic

6. Subsequent encounter due to helicopter crash causing injury to occupant
   V95.01xD Helicopter crash injuring occupant
   Index to External Cause: Crash, aircraft, helicopter

7. Tree accidentally falling on person
   W20.8xxA Other cause of strike by thrown, projected for falling object
   Index to External Cause: Tree falling on or hitting (accidentally) (person)

8. Injury from walking into lamppost, subsequent encounter
   W22.02xD Walked into lamppost
   Index: Walked into stationary object, lamppost

9. Struck by softball
   W21.07xA Struck by softball
   Index to External Cause: Struck, sport equipment, ball, softball

10. Evaluation of injury to foot by being skated over by sharp skate blades
    W21.32xA Struck by skate blades
    Index to External Causes: Struck, sports equipment, skate blades

Answers for Chapter 18: Factors Influencing Health Status and Contact with Health Services

Check Your Knowledge of ICD-10-CM

1. false
2. false
3. true
4. true
5. false

Coding

1. Carrier of typhoid
   Z22.0 Carrier of typhoid
   Index: Carrier, typhoid

2. Type AB, Rh-negative blood
   Z67.31 Type AB blood, Rh negative
   Index: Blood, type, AB, Rh negative

3. Patient seen in the office for a sports physical
   Z02.5 Encounter for examination for participation in sport
   Index: Examination, medical, sport competition

4. Screening for HPV
   Z11.51 Encounter for screening for human papillomavirus
   Index: Screening, human papillomavirus

5. Occupational exposure to dust
   Z57.2 Occupational exposure to dust
   Index: Exposure, occupational, dust

6. Problems related to child living in a group home
   Z62.22 Institutional upbringing
   Index: Problem (with) (related to), child, living in group home

7. Lack of adequate sleep
   Z72.820 Sleep deprivation
   Index: Lack of, sleep (adequate)

8. Underachievement in school

   Z55.3 Underachievement in school

   Index: Underachievement in school

9. History of estrogen therapy

   Z92.23 Personal history of estrogen therapy

   Index: History, personal, estrogen therapy

10. Encounter for checking of IUD

    Z30.431 Encounter for surveillance of intrauterine contraceptive device

    Index: Contraception, contraceptive, device, checking

Answers for Chapter 19: Transition from ICD-9-CM to ICD-10-CM

Coding

1. Open wound of the nose, initial visit
   ICD-9-CM: 873.20
   ICD-10-CM: S01.20xA

2. Congenital salivary fistula
   ICD-9-CM: 750.24
   ICD-10-CM: Q38.4

3. Acute tonsillitis
   ICD-9-CM: 463
   ICD-10-CM: J03.90

4. Collapsed lung
   ICD-9-CM: 518.0
   ICD-10-CM: J98.19

5. Lung mass
   ICD-9-CM: 786.6
   ICD-10-CM: R91.8

6. Bronchial stenosis
   ICD-9-CM: 519.19
   ICD-10-CM: J98.09

7. Chronic hepatitis C
   ICD-9-CM: 070.54
   ICD-10-CM: B18.2

8. Alcohol withdrawal
   ICD-9-CM: 291.81
   ICD-10-CM: F10.239

9. Panic disorder
   ICD-9-CM: 300.01
   ICD-10-CM: F41.0

10. Obsessive-compulsive disorder
    ICD-9-CM: 300.3
    ICD-10-CM: F42

Answers for Chapter 20: Coding with ICD-10-PCS

Alphabetic Index Exercise

1. See Drainage
2. See Dilation, Heart, and Great Vessels 027
3. See Excision
4. See Omentum, lesser
5. Use Nerve, Facial

PCS Table Exercise

1. 0NH00NZ (craniotomy is an open procedure)
2. 0NH03MZ

Section Exercise

1. __6__ Extracorporeal Therapies
2. __1__ Obstetrics
3. __2__ Placement
4. __G__ Mental Health
5. __H__ Substance Abuse Treatment

Body System Exercise

1. __D__ Right hemicolectomy
2. __P__ Scapulectomy
3. __8__ Dilation of left lacrimal duct
4. __6__ Percutaneous mechanical thrombectomy-femoral vein (thrombectomy—see Extirpation)
5. __F__ Laparoscopic cholecystectomy

Root Operation Exercise 1

1. Fragmentation
2. Extirpation

3. Drainage

4. Fragmentation

5. Extirpation

Root Operation Exercise 2

1. Alphabetic Index provides an entry under Resection, Stomach for the pylorus; therefore this would be classified as a Resection procedure. It is the coder's responsibility to translate the physician's documentation into PCS language; therefore, the physician states Excision is translated to Resection using PCS definitions. Coders would use the first four characters of 0DT7 to reference the PCS table and complete the code based on the approach and device/qualifier (if applicable).

2. Alphabetic Index provides an entry under Resection for the lingula of the bronchus; therefore, the correct four characters of the code are 0BT9. Removal is NOT the root operation.

3. There is no entry for Resection of the tail of the pancreas. This meets the definition of Excision (portion of body part)—there is no subdivision classification for resection of tail of pancreas in the Alphabetic Index. Refer to Excision in the Alphabetic Index for 0FBG.

Root Operation Exercise 3

1. Revision

2. Replacement

3. Dilation

4. Reposition

5. Drainage

Body Part Exercise 1

1. *use* Muscle, Foot, Left. Transfer, Muscle, Foot, Left—0KXW

2. *use* Nerve, Tibial. Excision, Nerve, Tibia—01BG

3. *use* Artery, Femoral, Right. Repair, Artery, Femoral, Right—04QK

Body Part Exercise 2

1. __8__ The surgeon excised a polyp from the first portion of the small intestine.

2. __4__ A biopsy was performed from the region of the stomach where it connects to the esophagus.

3. __C__ The surgeon states that there is a lesion located on the sphincter muscle that connects the small intestine to the large intestine.

Approach Exercise 1

1. Via natural or artificial opening endoscopic

2. Percutaneous

3. Open

4. Percutaneous endoscopic

5. Percutaneous

Approach Exercise 2

1. Via natural or artificial opening endoscopic

2. Open

3. External

4. Open

5. Via natural or artificial opening endoscopic

Approach Exercise 3

1. Percutaneous (right femoral artery was accessed). Further web research will reveal that the Seldinger technique uses a needle to access the artery.

2. Open (incision was opened over the patella)

3. Percutaneous endoscopic (umbilical incision made and Visiport introduced). Perform a web search on Visiport and it will reveal that it is an instrument used in laparoscopic procedures.

Device Exercise 1

1. Use Intraluminal Device

2. Use Synthetic Substitute

3. Use Cardiac Resynchronization Pacemaker Pulse Generator in 0JH

4. Use Synthetic Substitute

Device Exercise 2

1. Autologous tissue substitute
2. Synthetic substitute
3. Zooplastic tissue

Qualifier Case Study

Case Study

Answer: 0SRB02A Metal (titanium) on Plastic (Polyethylene). The Press Fit method is uncemented. Perform a web search for hip replacement methods for a full explanation of the types displayed in the PCS table.

Building an ICD-10-PCS Code

1. Bilateral liposuction of upper arms (elective procedure)
   0X083ZZ
   0X093ZZ

Character	Description
Section	Medical and Surgical
Body System	Anatomical Regions, Upper Extremities
Operation	Alteration
Body Part	Upper Arms (right-character 8) (left-character 9)
Approach	Percutaneous
Device	No Device
Qualifier	No Qualifier

   Index: No entry for Liposuction, apply definitions of Root Operation.

   Root Operation: Alteration

   Perform web research to determine how the procedure is performed: Percutaneous approach.

   Index: Alternation, Arm, Upper, Left 0X09 and Right 0X08

2. Laparoscopic-assisted total vaginal hysterectomy (LAVH)
   0UT9FZZ

Character	Description
Section	Medical and Surgical
Body System	Female Reproductive System
Operation	Resection
Body Part	Uterus
Approach	Via Natural or Artificial Opening with Percutaneous Endoscopic Assistance
Device	No Device
Qualifier	No Qualifier

   Index: Hysterectomy provides two choices: Excision and Resection

   Root Operation: Resection, Uterus 0UT9

   This is the only use of this type of approach. In the Operative Report, coders need to review the documentation to determine if the cervix and/or tubes and ovaries were also removed.

3. Advancement flap skin graft covering left forearm
   0HXEXZZ

Character	Description
Section	Medical and Surgical
Body System	Skin and Breast
Operation	Transfer
Body Part	Skin, Left Lower Arm
Approach	External
Device	No Device
Qualifier	No Qualifier

   Index: Advancement—see Reposition or see Transfer (advancement flap is a transfer since the original blood source is left intact)

   Index: Transfer, skin, Lower Arm, Left 0HXEXZZ

4. Open reduction with internal fixation, displaced left lateral ankle fracture

0SSG04Z

Character	Description
Section	Medical and Surgical
Body System	Lower Joints
Operation	Reposition
Body Part	Ankle Joint, Left
Approach	Open
Device	Internal Fixation Device
Qualifier	No Qualifier

Index: Reduction, Fracture—*see Reposition*

Index: Reposition, Joint, Ankle, Left 0SSG

5. ERCP with balloon dilation of common bile duct

0F798ZZ

Character	Description
Section	Medical and Surgical
Body System	Hepatobiliary System and Pancreas
Operation	Dilation
Body Part	Common Bile Duct
Approach	Via Natural or Artificial Opening Endoscopic
Device	No Device
Qualifier	No Qualifier

Index: Dilation, Duct, Common Bile 0F79

Note that the use of the balloon (device) is not assigned a character value. Official coding guideline (B6.1a) states that a device is coded only if a device remains after the procedure is completed. ERCP is the approach (endoscopic).

Operative Report 1

PROCEDURE PERFORMED: Right breast lumpectomy.

ICD-10-PCS Code(s)

0HBT0ZX Excision of Right Breast, Open Approach, Diagnostic

Coding Notes: Search for lumpectomy in the index for a reference to either "see Excision" or "see Resection." Apply definitions from the Root Operations. *Resection* is removal of ALL of a body part and *Excision* is cutting out a PORTION of a body part.

Index: Excision, breast, right 0HBT

Reference the table to build the remainder of the characters.

Operative Report 2

PROCEDURE PERFORMED: Open reduction and internal fixation of left distal radius.

ICD-10-PCS Code(s):

0PSJ04Z Reposition Left Radius with Internal Fixation Device, Open Approach

Index: Reduction, fracture—*see Reposition. Reposition, radius, left 0PSJ*

Reference the table to build the remainder of the characters.

Operative Report 3

PROCEDURE PERFORMED: Esophago-gastroduodenoscopy with cautery.

POSTOPERATIVE DIAGNOSES: Gastrointestinal (GI) bleed and angiodysplasia of the stomach.

ICD-10-PCS Code(s):

0D568ZZ Destruction of Stomach, Via Natural or Artificial Opening Endoscopic

Coding Notes: Use of cautery supports the definition of the Root Operation *Destruction*. Destruction is the physical eradication of all or a portion of a body part by the direct use of energy, force, or a destructive agent.

Index: Destruction, stomach 0D56

Reference the table to build the remainder of the characters.

Operative Report 4

PROCEDURE: Colonoscopy.

ICD-10-PCS Code(s):

0DJD8ZZ Inspection of Lower Intestinal Tract, Via Natural or Artificial Opening Endoscopic

Index: Colonoscopy 0DJD8ZZ

Coding Notes: In this case, the entire code is provided from the Index. Note that the Root Operation is *Inspection*.

Operative Report 5

POSTOPERATIVE DIAGNOSIS: Right nasal foreign body.

His nose was examined and a small cotton foreign body was removed from the anterior aspect of the nose.

ICD-10-PCS Code(s):

09CKXZZ Extirpation of Matter from Nose, External Approach

Coding Notes: In this case, coders must apply definitions for Root Operations to successfully use the Index. There is no entry for "removal of foreign body." *Extirpation* is the Root Operation. The definition is "taking or cutting out solid matter from a body part."

Index: *Extirpation, Nose 09CK*

Reference the table to build the remainder of the characters.

Answers for Chapter 21: Application of Coding Guidelines

1. A

   Guideline Section: I.C.19.e.5.b (Chapter 19: Injury/Poisonings)

2. B

   Guideline Section: I.C.19.e.5.a (Chapter 19: Injury/Poisonings)

3. B

   Guideline Section: II.I.1 (Selection of Principal Diagnosis)

4. D

   Guideline Section: II, A (Selection of Principal Diagnosis)

5. A

   Guideline Section: III.B (Reporting Additional Diagnoses)

6. B

   Guideline Section: I.C.19.b.1 (Chapter 19: Injury/Poisonings)

7. C

   Guideline Section: I.C.19.e.5 (Chapter 19: Injury/Poisonings)

8. B

   Guideline Section: I.C.15.n (Chapter 15: Pregnancy, Childbirth, and Puerperium)

9. A

   Guideline Section: I.C.19.c. (Chapter 19: Injury/Poisonings)

10. B

    Guideline Section: I.C.1.a.b (Chapter 1: Certain Infectious and Parasitic Diseases)

Answers for Chapter 22: Coding Case Studies

1. ICD-10-CM code(s): N85.8, D62

   ICD-10-PCS code(s): 0UDB8ZX

2. ICD-10-CM code(s): Z51.11, C50.911, Z90.11

3. ICD-10-CM code(s): K29.00, R03.0

4. ICD-10-CM code(s): K80.20

   ICD-10-PCS code(s): 0FT40ZZ, 0FJ44ZZ

5. ICD-10-CM code(s): R10.9

6. ICD-10-CM code(s): F10.231

7. ICD-10-CM code(s): J44.1

8. ICD-10-CM code(s): I20.0

9. ICD-10-CM code(s): S82.252A

   ICD-10-PCS code(s): 0QSH0ZZ

10. ICD-10-CM code(s): Z38.00, Q86.0

Answers for Chapter 23: Decision-Based Coding

Case Study 1

Coding Assignment	Rationale
ICD-10-CM Code(s): D18.01 Hemangioma of skin and subcutaneous tissue (correct)	Correct assignment
ICD-10-PCS Code(s): 0JBL0ZZ (incorrect) Excision of Right Upper Leg Subcutaneous Tissue and Fascia, Open Approach	The body part character should be M for left upper leg, not L for right upper leg Correct code assignment: **0JBM0ZZ** **Excision of Left Upper Leg Subcutaneous Tissue and Fascia, Open Approach**

Case Study 2

Coding Assignment	Rationale
ICD-10-CM Code(s): K80.50 Calculus of bile duct without cholangitis or cholecystitis without obstruction (correct)	Correct assignment
ICD-10-PCS Code(s): 0FT44ZZ (correct) Resection of Gallbladder, Percutaneous Endoscopic Approach	Correct assignment Resection of Gallbladder, Percutaneous Endoscopic Approach

Case Study 3

Coding Assignment	Rationale
ICD-10-CM Code(s): S82.201A Unspecified fracture of shaft of right tibia (incorrect)	The code is correct but the extension D should be assigned for subsequent encounter for closed fracture with routine healing. Correct code: **S82.201D**
ICD-10-PCS Code(s): 0QPGX4Z (incorrect) Removal of Internal Fixation Device from Right Tibia, External Approach	The approach character X is incorrect; it is an open approach. Correct code: **0QPG04Z** **Removal of Internal Fixation Device from Right Tibia, Open Approach**

Case Study 4

Coding Assignment	Rationale
ICD-10-CM Code(s): R13.10 Dysphagia, unspecified (correct) K21.9 Gastro-esophageal reflux disease without esophagitis (correct) K22.70 Barrett's esophagus without dysplasia (do not report)	The code selection for Dysphagia and GERD is correct. The code for Barrett's esophagus should not be reported according to coding guidelines. In an outpatient setting, a "rule out" diagnosis is not assigned a code. In this case, "rule out" means that the physician is considering the diagnosis but has not been confirmed.
ICD-10-PCS Code(s): 0DB38ZZ (incorrect) Excision of Lower Esophagus, Via Natural or Artificial Opening Endoscopic	Biopsies were taken for diagnostic purposes. The last character should be "X." Correct code: **0DB38ZX** **Excision of Lower Esophagus, Via Natural or Artificial Opening Endoscopic Approach**

Case Study 5

Coding Assignment	Rationale
ICD-10-CM Code(s): Z45.09 Encounter for adjustment and management of other cardiac device (correct) I49.9 Cardiac arrhythmia, unspecified (correct)	Correct assignment
ICD-10-PCS Code(s): 0WP80YZ (incorrect) Removal of Other Device from Chest Wall, Open Approach	Cardiac recorder lies directly under the skin. Index: Removal of device from—Subcutaneous Tissue and Fascia, Trunk Correct code assignment **0JPT0PZ** **Removal of Cardiac Rhythm-Related Device from Trunk Subcutaneous Tissue and Fascia, Open Approach**

Appendix B: Anatomical Diagrams

This appendix can be used by the student as a reference tool. A comprehensive understanding of human anatomy is essential for correct code assignment.

Lymphatic Circulation and Major Lymph Node Locations

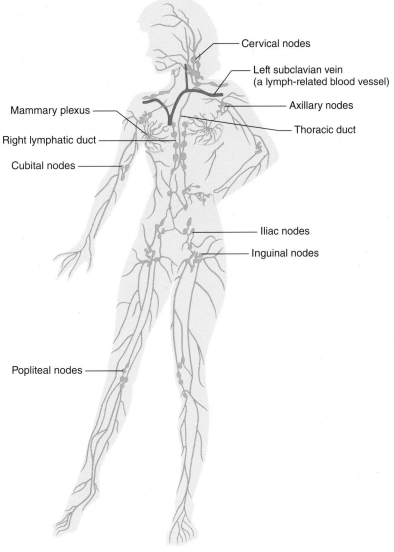

External View of the Heart

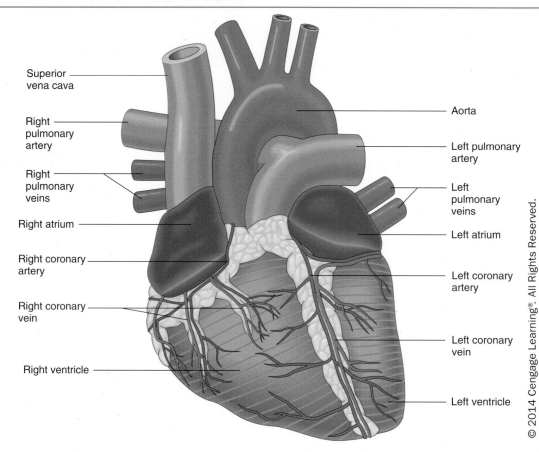

Superior vena cava

Right pulmonary artery

Right pulmonary veins

Right atrium

Right coronary artery

Right coronary vein

Right ventricle

Aorta

Left pulmonary artery

Left pulmonary veins

Left atrium

Left coronary artery

Left coronary vein

Left ventricle

Structures of the Gastrointestinal System

A.

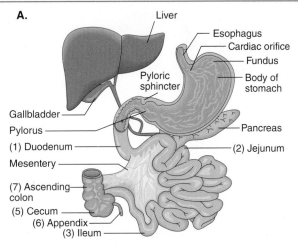

B.

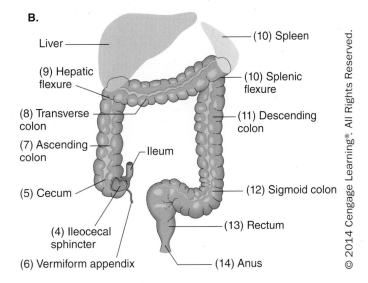

Endocrine Glands

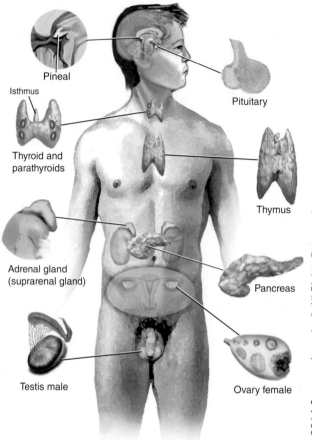

Pineal

Pituitary

Isthmus

Thyroid and parathyroids

Thymus

Adrenal gland (suprarenal gland)

Pancreas

Testis male

Ovary female

Structures of the Eyeball Shown in Cross-Section

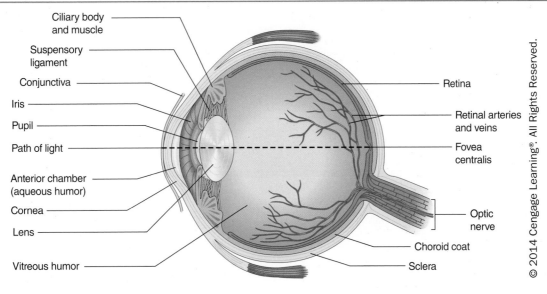

Ciliary body
and muscle

Suspensory
ligament

Conjunctiva

Iris

Pupil

Path of light

Anterior chamber
(aqueous humor)

Cornea

Lens

Vitreous humor

Retina

Retinal arteries
and veins

Fovea
centralis

Optic
nerve

Choroid coat

Sclera

Structures of the Ear Shown in Cross-Section

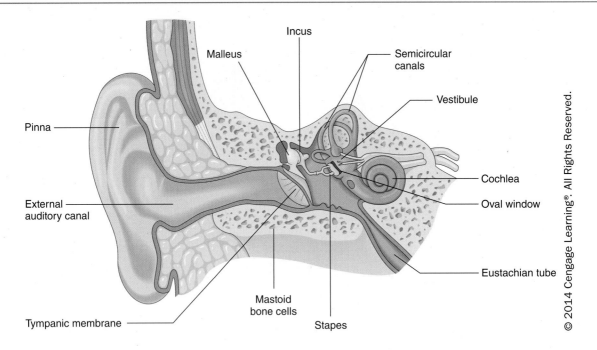

Pinna

External auditory canal

Tympanic membrane

Malleus

Incus

Semicircular canals

Vestibule

Cochlea

Oval window

Eustachian tube

Mastoid bone cells

Stapes

The Skin

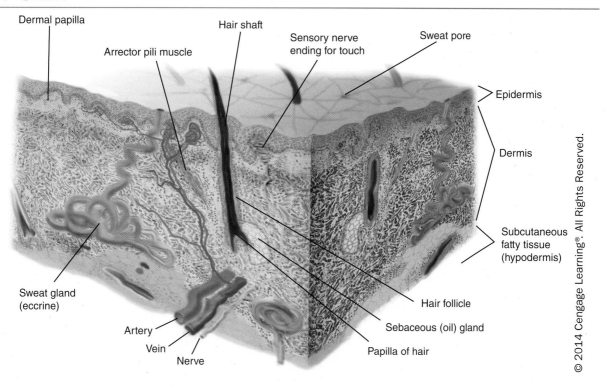

Dermal papilla

Arrector pili muscle

Hair shaft

Sensory nerve ending for touch

Sweat pore

Epidermis

Dermis

Subcutaneous fatty tissue (hypodermis)

Sweat gland (eccrine)

Artery

Vein

Nerve

Hair follicle

Sebaceous (oil) gland

Papilla of hair

Major Superficial Muscles of the Body: Anterior View

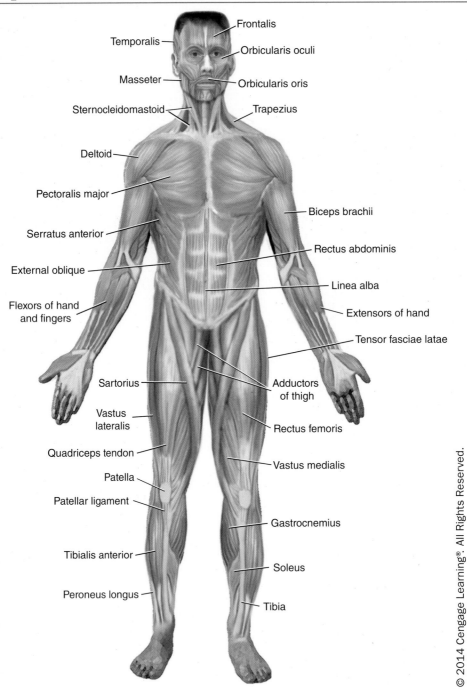

Frontalis

Temporalis

Orbicularis oculi

Masseter

Orbicularis oris

Sternocleidomastoid

Trapezius

Deltoid

Pectoralis major

Biceps brachii

Serratus anterior

Rectus abdominis

External oblique

Linea alba

Flexors of hand
and fingers

Extensors of hand

Tensor fasciae latae

Sartorius

Adductors
of thigh

Vastus
lateralis

Rectus femoris

Quadriceps tendon

Vastus medialis

Patella

Patellar ligament

Gastrocnemius

Tibialis anterior

Soleus

Peroneus longus

Tibia

Major Superficial Muscles of the Body: Posterior View

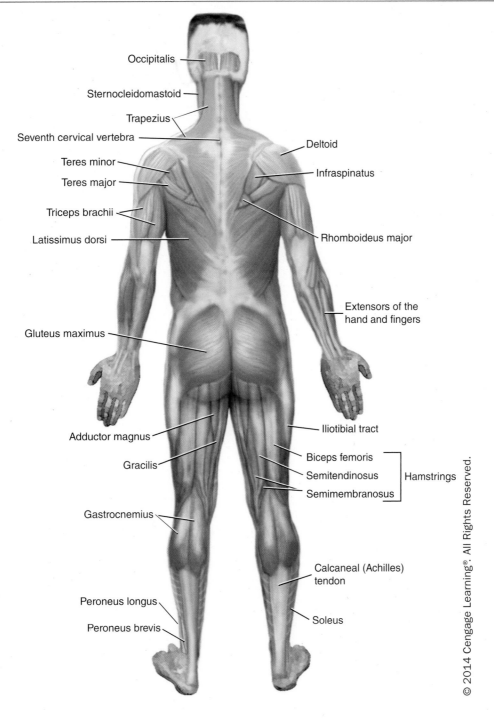

Occipitalis

Sternocleidomastoid

Trapezius

Seventh cervical vertebra

Teres minor

Teres major

Triceps brachii

Latissimus dorsi

Deltoid

Infraspinatus

Rhomboideus major

Extensors of the hand and fingers

Gluteus maximus

Adductor magnus

Gracilis

Gastrocnemius

Peroneus longus

Peroneus brevis

Iliotibial tract

Biceps femoris

Semitendinosus

Semimembranosus

Hamstrings

Calcaneal (Achilles) tendon

Soleus

Lateral View of the Brain

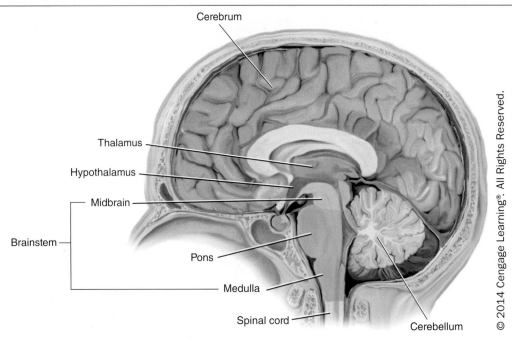

(A) internal brain structure

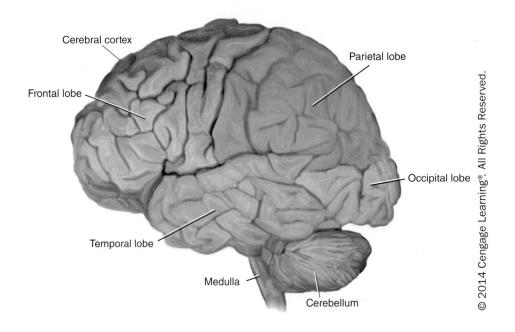

(B) external brain structure

Fetus in Position at Term

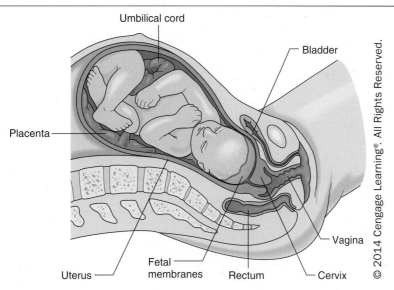

Umbilical cord

Bladder

Placenta

Uterus

Fetal membranes

Rectum

Vagina

Cervix

External Female Genitalia

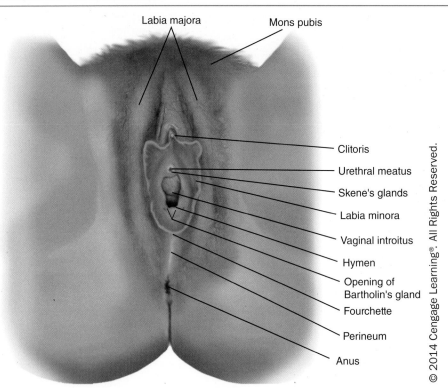

Labia majora

Mons pubis

Clitoris

Urethral meatus

Skene's glands

Labia minora

Vaginal introitus

Hymen

Opening of
Bartholin's gland

Fourchette

Perineum

Anus

Cross-Section of the Female Breast

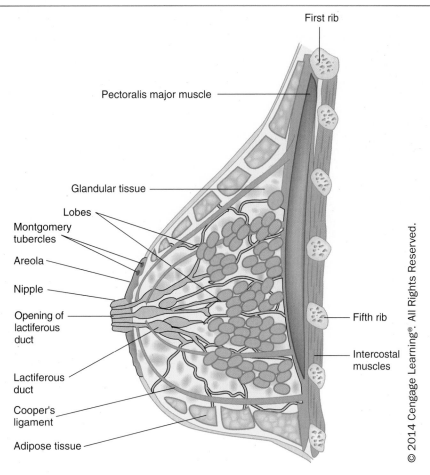

First rib

Pectoralis major muscle

Glandular tissue

Lobes

Montgomery tubercles

Areola

Nipple

Opening of lactiferous duct

Lactiferous duct

Cooper's ligament

Adipose tissue

Fifth rib

Intercostal muscles

Male Reproductive System

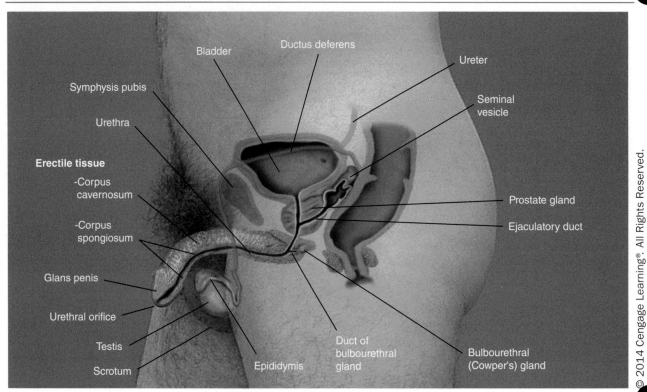

Structures of the Respiratory System

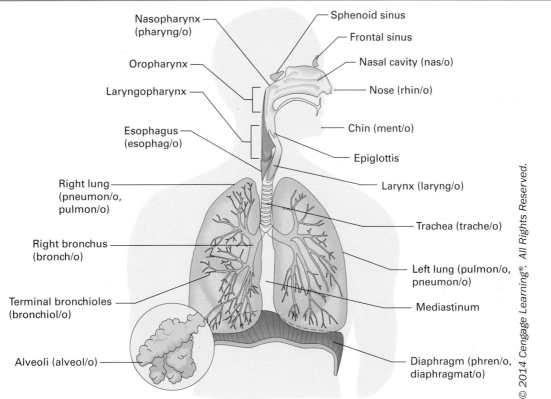

Nasopharynx (pharyng/o)

Oropharynx

Laryngopharynx

Esophagus (esophag/o)

Right lung (pneumon/o, pulmon/o)

Right bronchus (bronch/o)

Terminal bronchioles (bronchiol/o)

Alveoli (alveol/o)

Sphenoid sinus

Frontal sinus

Nasal cavity (nas/o)

Nose (rhin/o)

Chin (ment/o)

Epiglottis

Larynx (laryng/o)

Trachea (trache/o)

Left lung (pulmon/o, pneumon/o)

Mediastinum

Diaphragm (phren/o, diaphragmat/o)

Lateral View of the Adult Human Skeleton

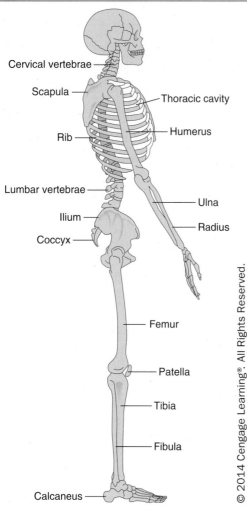

Cervical vertebrae

Scapula

Rib

Lumbar vertebrae

Ilium

Coccyx

Thoracic cavity

Humerus

Ulna

Radius

Femur

Patella

Tibia

Fibula

Calcaneus

Posterior View of the Human Skeleton

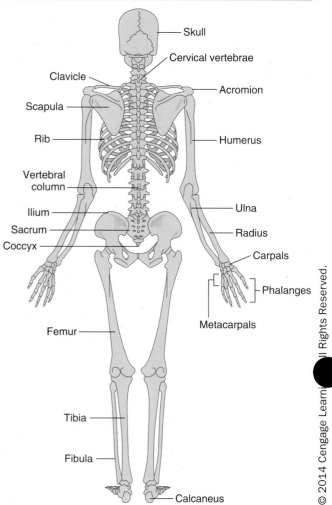

Skull

Cervical vertebrae

Clavicle

Acromion

Scapula

Rib

Humerus

Vertebral column

Ilium

Ulna

Sacrum

Radius

Coccyx

Carpals

Phalanges

Metacarpals

Femur

Tibia

Fibula

Calcaneus

⬤Urinary System

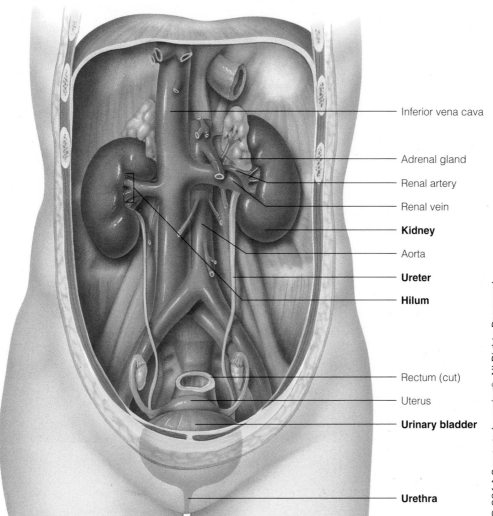

Inferior vena cava

Adrenal gland

Renal artery

Renal vein

Kidney

Aorta

Ureter

Hilum

Rectum (cut)

Uterus

Urinary bladder

Urethra

Division of the Abdomen into Quadrants

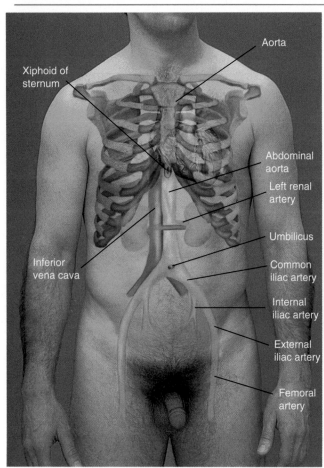

Aorta

Xiphoid of
sternum

Abdominal
aorta

Left renal
artery

Umbilicus

Inferior
vena cava

Common
iliac artery

Internal
iliac artery

External
iliac artery

Femoral
artery

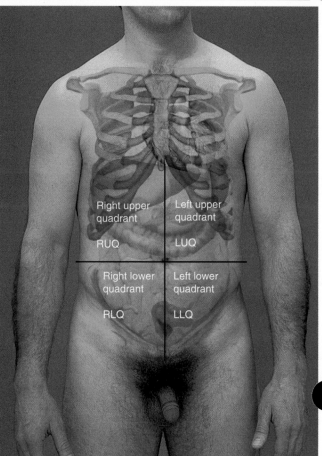

Right upper
quadrant

RUQ

Left upper
quadrant

LUQ

Right lower
quadrant

RLQ

Left lower
quadrant

LLQ

Directional Terms Relating to the Anatomical Position

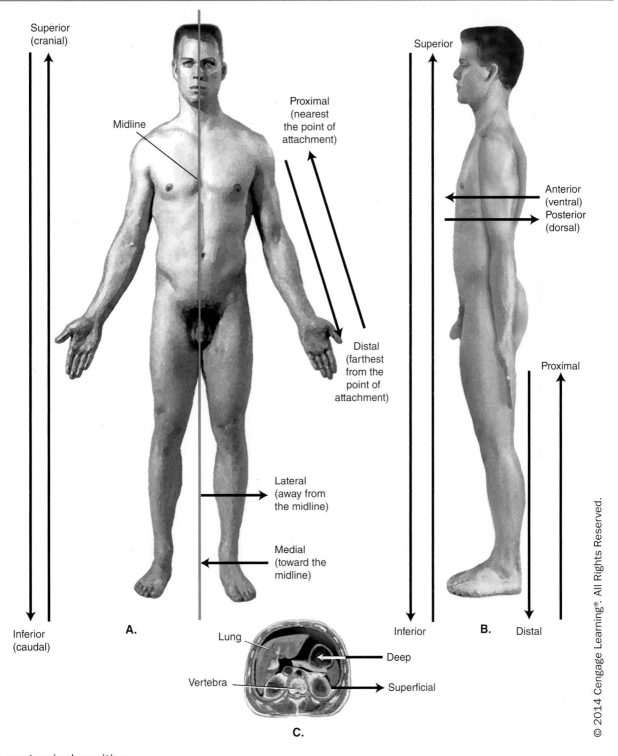

Superior
(cranial)

Midline

Proximal
(nearest
the point of
attachment)

Distal
(farthest
from the
point of
attachment)

Lateral
(away from
the midline)

Medial
(toward the
midline)

Inferior
(caudal)

A.

Lung

Vertebra

Deep

Superficial

C.

Superior

Anterior
(ventral)
Posterior
(dorsal)

Proximal

Inferior

B.   Distal

(A) anatomical position,
(B) lateral view of the body,
(C) directional terms deep and superficial

Appendix C: Definitions for Root Operations

Section 0—Medical and Surgical

Character 3—Operation	
Alteration	**Definition:** Modifying the anatomic structure of a body part without affecting the function of the body part **Explanation:** Principal purpose is to improve appearance **Includes/Examples:** Face lift, breast augmentation
Bypass	**Definition:** Altering the route of passage of the contents of a tubular body part **Explanation:** Rerouting contents of a body part to a downstream area of the normal route, to a similar route and body part, or to an abnormal route and dissimilar body part. Includes one or more anastomoses, with or without the use of a device **Includes/Examples:** Coronary artery bypass, colostomy formation
Change	**Definition:** Taking out or off a device from a body part and putting back an identical or similar device in or on the same body part without cutting or puncturing the skin or a mucous membrane **Explanation:** All CHANGE procedures are coded using the approach EXTERNAL **Includes/Examples:** Urinary catheter change, gastrostomy tube change
Control	**Definition:** Stopping, or attempting to stop, postprocedural bleeding **Explanation:** The site of the bleeding is coded as an anatomical region and not to a specific body part **Includes/Examples:** Control of post-prostatectomy hemorrhage, control of post-tonsillectomy hemorrhage
Creation	**Definition:** Making a new genital structure that does not take over the function of a body part **Explanation:** Used only for sex change operations **Includes/Examples:** Creation of vagina in a male, creation of penis in a female
Destruction	**Definition:** Physical eradication of all or a portion of a body part by the direct use of energy, force, or a destructive agent **Explanation:** None of the body part is physically taken out **Includes/Examples:** Fulguration of rectal polyp, cautery of skin lesion

(Continues)

Character 3—Operation (*Continued*)

Detachment	**Definition:** Cutting off all or a portion of the upper or lower extremities **Explanation:** The body part value is the site of the detachment, with a qualifier if applicable to further specify the level where the extremity was detached **Includes/Examples:** Below knee amputation, disarticulation of shoulder
Dilation	**Definition:** Expanding an orifice or the lumen of a tubular body part **Explanation:** The orifice can be a natural orifice or an artificially created orifice. Accomplished by stretching a tubular body part using intraluminal pressure or by cutting part of the orifice or wall of the tubular body part **Includes/Examples:** Percutaneous transluminal angioplasty, pyloromyotomy
Division	**Definition:** Cutting into a body part, without draining fluids and/or gases from the body part, in order to separate or transect a body part **Explanation:** All or a portion of the body part is separated into two or more portions **Includes/Examples:** Spinal cordotomy, osteotomy
Drainage	**Definition:** Taking or letting out fluids and/or gases from a body part **Explanation:** The qualifier DIAGNOSTIC is used to identify drainage procedures that are biopsies **Includes/Examples:** Thoracentesis, incision, and drainage
Excision	**Definition:** Cutting out or off, without replacement, a portion of a body part **Explanation:** The qualifier DIAGNOSTIC is used to identify excision procedures that are biopsies **Includes/Examples:** Partial nephrectomy, liver biopsy
Extirpation	**Definition:** Taking or cutting out solid matter from a body part **Explanation:** The solid matter may be an abnormal by-product of a biological function or a foreign body; it may be imbedded in a body part or in the lumen of a tubular body part. The solid matter may or may not have been previously broken into pieces **Includes/Examples:** Thrombectomy, choledocholithotomy
Extraction	**Definition:** Pulling or stripping out or off all or a portion of a body part by the use of force **Explanation:** The qualifier DIAGNOSTIC is used to identify extraction procedures that are biopsies **Includes/Examples:** Dilation and curettage, vein stripping

(*Continues*)

Character 3—Operation (*Continued*)

Fragmentation	**Definition:** Breaking solid matter in a body part into pieces **Explanation:** Physical force (e.g., manual, ultrasonic) applied directly or indirectly is used to break the solid matter into pieces. The solid matter may be an abnormal by-product of a biological function or a foreign body. The pieces of solid matter are not taken out **Includes/Examples:** Extracorporeal shockwave lithotripsy, transurethral lithotripsy
Fusion	**Definition:** Joining together portions of an articular body part rendering the articular body part immobile **Explanation:** The body part is joined together by fixation device, bone graft, or other means **Includes/Examples:** Spinal fusion, ankle arthrodesis
Insertion	**Definition:** Putting in a nonbiological appliance that monitors, assists, performs, or prevents a physiological function but does not physically take the place of a body part **Includes/Examples:** Insertion of radioactive implant, insertion of central venous catheter
Inspection	**Definition:** Visually and/or manually exploring a body part **Explanation:** Visual exploration may be performed with or without optical instrumentation. Manual exploration may be performed directly or through intervening body layers **Includes/Examples:** Diagnostic arthroscopy, exploratory laparotomy
Map	**Definition:** Locating the route of passage of electrical impulses and/or locating functional areas in a body part **Explanation:** Applicable only to the cardiac conduction mechanism and the central nervous system **Includes/Examples:** Cardiac mapping, cortical mapping
Occlusion	**Definition:** Completely closing an orifice or the lumen of a tubular body part **Explanation:** The orifice can be a natural orifice or an artificially created orifice **Includes/Examples:** Fallopian tube ligation, ligation of inferior vena cava
Reattachment	**Definition:** Putting back in or on all or a portion of a separated body part to its normal location or other suitable location **Explanation:** Vascular circulation and nervous pathways may or may not be reestablished **Includes/Examples:** Reattachment of hand, reattachment of avulsed kidney

(Continues)

Character 3—Operation (*Continued*)

Release	**Definition:** Freeing a body part from an abnormal physical constraint
	Explanation: Some of the restraining tissue may be taken out but none of the body part is taken out
	Includes/Examples: Adhesiolysis, carpal tunnel release
Removal	**Definition:** Taking out or off a device from a body part
	Explanation: If a device is taken out and a similar device put in without cutting or puncturing the skin or mucous membrane, the procedure is coded to the root operation CHANGE. Otherwise, the procedure for taking out a device is coded to the root operation REMOVAL
	Includes/Examples: Drainage tube removal, cardiac pacemaker removal
Repair	**Definition:** Restoring, to the extent possible, a body part to its normal anatomic structure and function
	Explanation: Used only when the method to accomplish the repair is not one of the other root operations
	Includes/Examples: Colostomy takedown, suture of laceration
Replacement	**Definition:** Putting in or on biological or synthetic material that physically takes the place and/or function of all or a portion of a body part
	Explanation: The body part may have been taken out or replaced, or may be taken out, physically eradicated, or rendered nonfunctional during the Replacement procedure. A Removal procedure is coded for taking out the device used in a previous replacement procedure
	Includes/Examples: Total hip replacement, bone graft, free skin graft
Reposition	**Definition:** Moving to its normal location, or other suitable location, all or a portion of a body part
	Explanation: The body part is moved to a new location from an abnormal location, or from a normal location where it is not functioning correctly. The body part may or may not be cut out or off to be moved to the new location
	Includes/Examples: Reposition of undescended testicle, fracture reduction
Resection	**Definition:** Cutting out or off, without replacement, all of a body part
	Includes/Examples: Total nephrectomy, total lobectomy of lung
Restriction	**Definition:** Partially closing an orifice or the lumen of a tubular body part
	Explanation: The orifice can be a natural orifice or an artificially created orifice
	Includes/Examples: Esophagogastric fundoplication, cervical cerclage

(*Continues*)

Character 3—Operation (*Continued*)

Revision	**Definition:** Correcting, to the extent possible, a portion of a malfunctioning device or the position of a displaced device **Explanation:** Revision can include correcting a malfunctioning or displaced device by taking out and/or putting in part of the device **Includes/Examples:** Adjustment of position of pacemaker lead, recementing of hip prosthesis
Supplement	**Definition:** Putting in or on biological or synthetic material that physically reinforces and/or augments the function of a portion of a body part **Explanation:** The biological material is nonliving, or is living and from the same individual. The body part may have been previously replaced, and the Supplement procedure is performed to physically reinforce and/or augment the function of the replaced body part **Includes/Examples:** Herniorrhaphy using mesh, free nerve graft, mitral valve ring annuloplasty put a new acetabular liner in a previous hip replacement
Transfer	**Definition:** Moving, without taking out, all or a portion of a body part to another location to take over the function of all or a portion of a body part **Explanation:** The body part transferred remains connected to its vascular and nervous supply **Includes/Examples:** Tendon transfer, skin pedicle flap transfer
Transplantation	**Definition:** Putting in or on all or a portion of a living body part taken from another individual or animal to physically take the place and/or function of all or a portion of a similar body part **Explanation:** The native body part may or may not be taken out, and the transplanted body part may take over all or a portion of its function **Includes/Examples:** Kidney transplant, heart transplant

Permission to reuse in accordance with http://www.cms.hhs.gov Content Reuse Policy

Appendix D: ICD-10-PCS Coding Guidelines

ICD-10-PCS Official Guidelines for Coding

and Reporting

2013

The Centers for Medicare and Medicaid Services (CMS) and the National Center for Health Statistics (NCHS), two departments within the U.S. Federal Government's Department of Health and Human Services (DHHS) provide the following guidelines for coding and reporting using the International Classification of Diseases, 10th Revision, Procedure Coding System (ICD-10-PCS). These guidelines should be used as a companion document to the official version of the ICD-10-PCS as published on the CMS website. The ICD-10-PCS is a procedure classification published by the United States for classifying procedures performed in hospital inpatient health care settings.

These guidelines have been approved by the four organizations that make up the Cooperating Parties for the ICD-10-PCS: the American Hospital Association (AHA), the American Health Information Management Association (AHIMA), CMS, and NCHS.

These guidelines are a set of rules that have been developed to accompany and complement the official conventions and instructions provided within the ICD-10-PCS itself. The instructions and conventions of the classification take precedence over guidelines. These guidelines are based on the coding and sequencing instructions in the Tables, Index and Definitions of ICD-10-PCS, but provide additional instruction. Adherence to these guidelines when assigning ICD-10-PCS procedure codes is required under the Health Insurance Portability and Accountability Act (HIPAA). The procedure codes have been adopted under HIPAA for hospital inpatient healthcare settings. A joint effort between the healthcare provider and the coder is essential to achieve complete and accurate documentation, code assignment, and reporting of diagnoses and procedures. These guidelines have been developed to assist both the healthcare provider and the coder in identifying those procedures that are to be reported. The importance of consistent, complete documentation in the medical record cannot be overemphasized. Without such documentation accurate coding cannot be achieved.

Table of Contents

Conventions

A1

ICD-10-PCS codes are composed of seven characters. Each character is an axis of classification that specifies information about the procedure performed. Within a defined code range, a character specifies the same type of information in that axis of classification.

Example: The fifth axis of classification specifies the approach in sections 0 through 4 and 7 through 9 of the system.

A2

One of 34 possible values can be assigned to each axis of classification in the seven-character code: they are the numbers 0 through 9 and the alphabet (except I and O because they are easily confused with the numbers 1 and 0). The number of unique values used in an axis of classification differs as needed.

Example: Where the fifth axis of classification specifies the approach, seven different approach values are currently used to specify the approach.

A3

The valid values for an axis of classification can be added to as needed.

Example: If a significantly distinct type of device is used in a new procedure, a new device value can be added to the system.

A4

As with words in their context, the meaning of any single value is a combination of its axis of classification and any preceding values on which it may be dependent.

Example: The meaning of a body part value in the Medical and Surgical section is always dependent on the body system value. The body part value 0 in the Central Nervous body system specifies Brain and the body part value 0 in the Peripheral Nervous body system specifies Cervical Plexus.

A5

As the system is expanded to become increasingly detailed, over time more values will depend on preceding values for their meaning.

Example: In the Lower Joints body system, the device value 3 in the root operation Insertion specifies Infusion Device and the device value 3 in the root operation Replacement specifies Ceramic Synthetic Substitute.

A6

The purpose of the alphabetic index is to locate the appropriate table that contains all information necessary to construct a procedure code. The PCS Tables should always be consulted to find the most appropriate valid code.

A7

It is not required to consult the index first before proceeding to the tables to complete the code. A valid code may be chosen directly from the tables.

A8

All seven characters must be specified to be a valid code. If the documentation is incomplete for coding purposes, the physician should be queried for the necessary information.

A9

Within a PCS table, valid codes include all combinations of choices in characters 4 through 7 contained in the same row of the table. In the example below, 0JHT3VZ is a valid code, and 0JHW3VZ is *not* a valid code.

Section: 0 Medical and Surgical
Body System: J Subcutaneous Tissue and Fascia
Operation: H Insertion: Putting in a nonbiological appliance that monitors, assists, performs, or prevents a physiological function but does not physically take the place of a body part

Body Part	Approach	Device	Qualifier
S Subcutaneous Tissue and Fascia, Head and Neck V Subcutaneous Tissue and Fascia, Upper Extremity W Subcutaneous Tissue and Fascia, Lower Extremity	0 Open 3 Percutaneous	1 Radioactive Element 3 Infusion Device	Z No Qualifier
T Subcutaneous Tissue and Fascia, Trunk	0 Open 3 Percutaneous	1 Radioactive Element 3 Infusion Device V Infusion Pump	Z No Qualifier

A10

"And," when used in a code description, means "and/or."
Example: Lower Arm and Wrist Muscle means lower arm and/or wrist muscle.

A11

Many of the terms used to construct PCS codes are defined within the system. It is the coder's responsibility to determine what the documentation in the medical record equates to in the PCS definitions. The physician is not expected to use the terms used in PCS code descriptions, nor is the coder required to query the physician when the correlation between the documentation and the defined PCS terms is clear.
Example: When the physician documents "partial resection" the coder can independently correlate "partial resection" to the root operation Excision without querying the physician for clarification.

Medical and Surgical Section Guidelines (section 0)

B2. Body System

General guidelines

B2.1a

The procedure codes in the general anatomical regions body systems should only be used when the procedure is performed on an anatomical region rather than a specific body part (e.g., root operations Control and Detachment, Drainage of a body cavity) or on the rare occasion when no information is available to support assignment of a code to a specific body part.

Example: Control of postoperative hemorrhage is coded to the root operation Control found in the general anatomical regions body systems.

B2.1b

Where the general body part values "upper" and "lower" are provided as an option in the Upper Arteries, Lower Arteries, Upper Veins, Lower Veins, Muscles and Tendons body systems, "upper" or "lower "specifies body parts located above or below the diaphragm respectively.

Example: Vein body parts above the diaphragm are found in the Upper Veins body system; vein body parts below the diaphragm are found in the Lower Veins body system.

B3. Root Operation

General guidelines
B3.1a
In order to determine the appropriate root operation, the full definition of the root operation as contained in the PCS Tables must be applied.

B3.1b
Components of a procedure specified in the root operation definition and explanation are not coded separately. Procedural steps necessary to reach the operative site and close the operative site, including anastomosis of a tubular body part, are also not coded separately. *Example*: Resection of a joint as part of a joint replacement procedure is included in the root operation definition of Replacement and is not coded separately. Laparotomy performed to reach the site of an open liver biopsy is not coded separately. In a resection of sigmoid colon with anastomosis of descending colon to rectum, the anastomosis is not coded separately.

Multiple procedures
B3.2
During the same operative episode, multiple procedures are coded if:
a.   The same root operation is performed on different body parts as defined by distinct values of the body part character.
        Example: Diagnostic excision of liver and pancreas are coded separately.
b.   The same root operation is repeated at different body sites that are included in the same body part value.
        Example: Excision of the sartorius muscle and excision of the gracilis muscle are both included in the upper leg muscle body part value, and multiple procedures are coded.
c.   Multiple root operations with distinct objectives are performed on the same body part.
        Example: Destruction of sigmoid lesion and bypass of sigmoid colon are coded separately.
d.   The intended root operation is attempted using one approach, but is converted to a different approach.
        Example: Laparoscopic cholecystectomy converted to an open cholecystectomy is coded as percutaneous endoscopic Inspection and open Resection.

Discontinued procedures
B3.3
If the intended procedure is discontinued, code the procedure to the root operation performed. If a procedure is discontinued before any other root operation is performed, code the root operation Inspection of the body part or anatomical region inspected.
Example: A planned aortic valve replacement procedure is discontinued after the initial thoracotomy and before any incision is made in the heart muscle, when the patient

becomes hemodynamically unstable. This procedure is coded as an open Inspection of the mediastinum.

Biopsy followed by more definitive treatment
B3.4
If a diagnostic Excision, Extraction, or Drainage procedure (biopsy) is followed by a more definitive procedure, such as Destruction, Excision or Resection at the same procedure site, both the biopsy and the more definitive treatment are coded.
Example: Biopsy of breast followed by partial mastectomy at the same procedure site, both the biopsy and the partial mastectomy procedure are coded.

Overlapping body layers
B3.5
If the root operations Excision, Repair or Inspection are performed on overlapping layers of the musculoskeletal system, the body part specifying the deepest layer is coded.
Example: Excisional debridement that includes skin and subcutaneous tissue and muscle is coded to the muscle body part.

Bypass procedures
B3.6a
Bypass procedures are coded by identifying the body part bypassed "from" and the body part bypassed "to." The fourth character body part specifies the body part bypassed from, and the qualifier specifies the body part bypassed to.
Example: Bypass from stomach to jejunum, stomach is the body part and jejunum is the qualifier.

B3.6b
Coronary arteries are classified by number of distinct sites treated, rather than number of coronary arteries or anatomic name of a coronary artery (e.g., left anterior descending). Coronary artery bypass procedures are coded differently than other bypass procedures as described in the previous guideline. Rather than identifying the body part bypassed from, the body part identifies the number of coronary artery sites bypassed to, and the qualifier specifies the vessel bypassed from.
Example: Aortocoronary artery bypass of one site on the left anterior descending coronary artery and one site on the obtuse marginal coronary artery is classified in the body part axis of classification as two coronary artery sites and the qualifier specifies the aorta as the body part bypassed from.

B3.6c
If multiple coronary artery sites are bypassed, a separate procedure is coded for each coronary artery site that uses a different device and/or qualifier.
Example: Aortocoronary artery bypass and internal mammary coronary artery bypass are coded separately.

Control vs. more definitive root operations
B3.7

The root operation Control is defined as, "Stopping, or attempting to stop, postprocedural bleeding." If an attempt to stop postprocedural bleeding is initially unsuccessful, and to stop the bleeding requires performing any of the definitive root operations Bypass, Detachment, Excision, Extraction, Reposition, Replacement, or Resection, then that root operation is coded instead of Control.
Example: Resection of spleen to stop postprocedural bleeding is coded to Resection instead of Control.

Excision vs. Resection
B3.8
PCS contains specific body parts for anatomical subdivisions of a body part, such as lobes of the lungs or liver and regions of the intestine. Resection of the specific body part is coded whenever all of the body part is cut out or off, rather than coding Excision of a less specific body part.
Example: Left upper lung lobectomy is coded to Resection of Upper Lung Lobe, Left rather than Excision of Lung, Left.

Excision for graft
B3.9
If an autograft is obtained from a different body part in order to complete the objective of the procedure, a separate procedure is coded.
Example: Coronary bypass with excision of saphenous vein graft, excision of saphenous vein is coded separately.

Fusion procedures of the spine
B3.10a
The body part coded for a spinal vertebral joint(s) rendered immobile by a spinal fusion procedure is classified by the level of the spine (e.g. thoracic). There are distinct body part values for a single vertebral joint and for multiple vertebral joints at each spinal level.
Example: Body part values specify Lumbar Vertebral Joint, Lumbar Vertebral Joints, 2 or More and Lumbosacral Vertebral Joint.

B3.10b
If multiple vertebral joints are fused, a separate procedure is coded for each vertebral joint that uses a different device and/or qualifier.
Example: Fusion of lumbar vertebral joint, posterior approach, anterior column and fusion of lumbar vertebral joint, posterior approach, posterior column are coded separately.

B3.10c
Combinations of devices and materials are often used on a vertebral joint to render the joint immobile. When combinations of devices are used on the same vertebral joint, the device value coded for the procedure is as follows:

- If an interbody fusion device is used to render the joint immobile (alone or containing other material like bone graft), the procedure is coded with the device value Interbody Fusion Device
- If bone graft is the *only* device used to render the joint immobile, the procedure is coded with the device value Nonautologous Tissue Substitute or Autologous Tissue Substitute
- If a mixture of autologous and nonautologous bone graft (with or without biological or synthetic extenders or binders) is used to render the joint immobile, code the procedure with the device value Autologous Tissue Substitute

Examples: Fusion of a vertebral joint using a cage style interbody fusion device containing morsellized bone graft is coded to the device Interbody Fusion Device.
Fusion of a vertebral joint using a bone dowel interbody fusion device made of cadaver bone and packed with a mixture of local morsellized bone and demineralized bone matrix is coded to the device Interbody Fusion Device.
Fusion of a vertebral joint using both autologous bone graft and bone bank bone graft is coded to the device Autologous Tissue Substitute.

Inspection procedures
B3.11a
Inspection of a body part(s) performed in order to achieve the objective of a procedure is not coded separately.
Example: Fiberoptic bronchoscopy performed for irrigation of bronchus, only the irrigation procedure is coded.

B3.11b
If multiple tubular body parts are inspected, the most distal body part inspected is coded. If multiple non-tubular body parts in a region are inspected, the body part that specifies the entire area inspected is coded.
Examples: Cystoureteroscopy with inspection of bladder and ureters is coded to the ureter body part value.
Exploratory laparotomy with general inspection of abdominal contents is coded to the peritoneal cavity body part value.

B3.11c
When both an Inspection procedure and another procedure are performed on the same body part during the same episode, if the Inspection procedure is performed using a different approach than the other procedure, the Inspection procedure is coded separately.
Example: Endoscopic Inspection of the duodenum is coded separately when open Excision of the duodenum is performed during the same procedural episode.

Occlusion vs. Restriction for vessel embolization procedures
B3.12
If the objective of an embolization procedure is to completely close a vessel, the root operation Occlusion is coded. If the objective of an embolization procedure is to narrow the lumen of a vessel, the root operation Restriction is coded.

Examples: Tumor embolization is coded to the root operation Occlusion, because the objective of the procedure is to cut off the blood supply to the vessel.
Embolization of a cerebral aneurysm is coded to the root operation Restriction, because the objective of the procedure is not to close off the vessel entirely, but to narrow the lumen of the vessel at the site of the aneurysm where it is abnormally wide.

Release procedures
B3.13
In the root operation Release, the body part value coded is the body part being freed and not the tissue being manipulated or cut to free the body part.
Example: Lysis of intestinal adhesions is coded to the specific intestine body part value.

Release vs. Division
B3.14
If the sole objective of the procedure is freeing a body part without cutting the body part, the root operation is Release. If the sole objective of the procedure is separating or transecting a body part, the root operation is Division.
Examples: Freeing a nerve root from surrounding scar tissue to relieve pain is coded to the root operation Release. Severing a nerve root to relieve pain is coded to the root operation Division.

Reposition for fracture treatment
B3.15
Reduction of a displaced fracture is coded to the root operation Reposition and the application of a cast or splint in conjunction with the Reposition procedure is not coded separately. Treatment of a nondisplaced fracture is coded to the procedure performed.
Examples: Putting a pin in a nondisplaced fracture is coded to the root operation Insertion.
Casting of a nondisplaced fracture is coded to the root operation Immobilization in the Placement section.

Transplantation vs. Administration
B3.16
Putting in a mature and functioning living body part taken from another individual or animal is coded to the root operation Transplantation. Putting in autologous or nonautologous cells is coded to the Administration section.
Example: Putting in autologous or nonautologous bone marrow, pancreatic islet cells or stem cells is coded to the Administration section.

B4. Body Part

General guidelines
B4.1a
If a procedure is performed on a portion of a body part that does not have a separate body part value, code the body part value corresponding to the whole body part.
Example: A procedure performed on the alveolar process of the mandible is coded to the mandible body part.

B4.1b
If the prefix "peri" is combined with a body part to identify the site of the procedure, the procedure is coded to the body part named.
Example: A procedure site identified as perirenal is coded to the kidney body part.

Branches of body parts
B4.2
Where a specific branch of a body part does not have its own body part value in PCS, the body part is coded to the closest proximal branch that has a specific body part value.
Example: A procedure performed on the mandibular branch of the trigeminal nerve is coded to the trigeminal nerve body part value.

Bilateral body part values
B4.3
Bilateral body part values are available for a limited number of body parts. If the identical procedure is performed on contralateral body parts, and a bilateral body part value exists for that body part, a single procedure is coded using the bilateral body part value. If no bilateral body part value exists, each procedure is coded separately using the appropriate body part value.
Example: The identical procedure performed on both fallopian tubes is coded once using the body part value Fallopian Tube, Bilateral. The identical procedure performed on both knee joints is coded twice using the body part values Knee Joint, Right and Knee Joint, Left.

Coronary arteries
B4.4
The coronary arteries are classified as a single body part that is further specified by number of sites treated and not by name or number of arteries. Separate body part values are used to specify the number of sites treated when the same procedure is performed on multiple sites in the coronary arteries.
Examples: Angioplasty of two distinct sites in the left anterior descending coronary artery with placement of two stents is coded as Dilation of Coronary Arteries, Two Sites, with Intraluminal Device.
Angioplasty of two distinct sites in the left anterior descending coronary artery, one with stent placed and one without, is coded separately as Dilation of Coronary Artery, One Site with Intraluminal Device, and Dilation of Coronary Artery, One Site with no device.

Tendons, ligaments, bursae and fascia near a joint
B4.5
Procedures performed on tendons, ligaments, bursae and fascia supporting a joint are coded to the body part in the respective body system that is the focus of the procedure. Procedures performed on joint structures themselves are coded to the body part in the joint body systems.
Example: Repair of the anterior cruciate ligament of the knee is coded to the knee bursae and ligament body part in the bursae and ligaments body system. Knee arthroscopy with shaving of articular cartilage is coded to the knee joint body part in the Lower Joints body system.

Skin, subcutaneous tissue and fascia overlying a joint
B4.6
If a procedure is performed on the skin, subcutaneous tissue or fascia overlying a joint, the procedure is coded to the following body part:
- Shoulder is coded to Upper Arm
- Elbow is coded to Lower Arm
- Wrist is coded to Lower Arm
- Hip is coded to Upper Leg
- Knee is coded to Lower Leg
- Ankle is coded to Foot

Fingers and toes
B4.7
If a body system does not contain a separate body part value for fingers, procedures performed on the fingers are coded to the body part value for the hand. If a body system does not contain a separate body part value for toes, procedures performed on the toes are coded to the body part value for the foot.
Example: Excision of finger muscle is coded to one of the hand muscle body part values in the Muscles body system.

B4.8
In the Gastrointestinal body system, the general body part values Upper Intestinal Tract and Lower Intestinal Tract are provided as an option for the root operations Change, Inspection, Removal and Revision. Upper Intestinal Tract includes the portion of the gastrointestinal tract from the esophagus down to and including the duodenum, and Lower Intestinal Tract includes the portion of the gastrointestinal tract from the jejunum down to and including the rectum and anus.
Example: In the root operation Change table, change of a device in the jejunum is coded using the body part Lower Intestinal Tract.

B5. Approach

Open approach with percutaneous endoscopic assistance
B5.2
Procedures performed using the open approach with percutaneous endoscopic assistance are coded to the approach Open.
Example: Laparoscopic-assisted sigmoidectomy is coded to the approach Open.

External approach
B5.3a
Procedures performed within an orifice on structures that are visible without the aid of any instrumentation are coded to the approach External.
Example: Resection of tonsils is coded to the approach External.

B5.3b
Procedures performed indirectly by the application of external force through the intervening body layers are coded to the approach External.
Example: Closed reduction of fracture is coded to the approach External.

Percutaneous procedure via device
B5.4
Procedures performed percutaneously via a device placed for the procedure are coded to the approach Percutaneous.
Example: Fragmentation of kidney stone performed via percutaneous nephrostomy is coded to the approach Percutaneous.

B6. Device

B6.1a
A device is coded only if a device remains after the procedure is completed. If no device remains, the device value No Device is coded.

B6.1b
Materials such as sutures, ligatures, radiological markers and temporary post-operative wound drains are considered integral to the performance of a procedure and are not coded as devices.

B6.1c
Procedures performed on a device only and not on a body part are specified in the root operations Change, Irrigation, Removal and Revision, and are coded to the procedure performed.
Example: Irrigation of percutaneous nephrostomy tube is coded to the root operation Irrigation of indwelling device in the Administration section.

Drainage device
B6.2
A separate procedure to put in a drainage device is coded to the root operation Drainage with the device value Drainage Device.

C. Obstetrics Section

Products of conception
C1
Procedures performed on the products of conception are coded to the Obstetrics section. Procedures performed on the pregnant female other than the products of conception are coded to the appropriate root operation in the Medical and Surgical section.
Example: Amniocentesis is coded to the products of conception body part in the Obstetrics section. Repair of obstetric urethral laceration is coded to the urethra body part in the Medical and Surgical section.

Procedures following delivery or abortion
C2
Procedures performed following a delivery or abortion for curettage of the endometrium or evacuation of retained products of conception are all coded in the Obstetrics section, to the root operation Extraction and the body part Products of Conception, Retained. Diagnostic or therapeutic dilation and curettage performed during times other than the postpartum or post-abortion period are all coded in the Medical and Surgical section, to the root operation Extraction and the body part Endometrium.